# Trusted Steward

## Moving Toward Total Stewardship

### Calvin T. Partain

Woman's Missionary Union®
Birmingham, Alabama

Woman's Missionary Union
P. O. Box 830010
Birmingham, Alabama 35283-0010

Dewey Decimal Classification: 248.4

Subject Headings: CHRISTIAN LIFE
                  STEWARDSHIP
                  SPIRITUAL LIFE

ISBN: 1-56309-162-3

W963101•0403•2M3

# Contents

# INTRODUCTION

As we ate lunch, George and Varena shared with us that they placed their possessions in trust with their state Baptist Foundation. The Foundation will pay them a monthly sum as long as they live. After their death, their children will receive proceeds from the trust until they have realized 110 percent of the original trust. Then it will be used by the Foundation to promote the work of the kingdom of God. George and Varena have firm trust that the Foundation will be faithful stewards of their entire estate.

The story is told about a wealthy building contractor who said to his superintendent, "I'm going on a world tour. While I am away, I want you to build me a house. Spare no expense. I want you to choose the design and the materials so I will have a pleasant surprise when I return."

The contractor left and the superintendent set about building the house. Unfortunately, he decided to use inferior, cheaper materials in places where it would not be seen and personally pocket the savings. The house looked beautiful, but the construction was shoddy. When the contractor returned, the superintendent took him to see the new house. At the end of the tour the contractor handed the house keys to the superintendent. "You have worked 25 years for me, and I wanted to reward you. This is your house."

"What do you have that you did not receive?" (1 Cor. 4:7 NIV). We have received, in trust from God, everything we have: body, mind, abilities, time, relationships, possessions, heritage, position, and the gospel of salvation. God has made us responsible for managing this trust. We have considerable freedom in this management. We can even choose to disregard His will and manage them selfishly. However, at His return we will give an accounting of how we handled our responsibility. Our eternal reward will be determined by our faithfulness.

Think of the trust God has placed in us! Jesus has trusted His property to us (Matt. 25:14). What kind of steward do you choose to be?

*A*gain, it will be like a man going on a journey, who called his servants and entrusted his property to them. To one he gave five talents of money, to another two talents, and to another one talent, each according to his ability. Then he went on his journey. The man who had received the five talents went at once and put his money to work and gained five more. So also, the one with the two talents gained two more. But the man who had received the one talent went off, dug a hole in the ground and hid his master's money. After a long time the master of those servants returned and settled accounts with them. The man who had received the five talents brought the other five. 'Master,' he said, 'you entrusted me with five talents. See, I have gained five more.' His master replied, 'Well done, good and faithful servant! You have been faithful with a few things; I will put you in charge of many things. Come and share your master's happiness!' The man with the two talents also came. 'Master,' he said, 'you entrusted me with two talents; see, I have gained two more.' His master replied, 'Well done, good and faithful servant! You have been faithful with a few things; I will put you in charge of many things. Come and share your master's happiness!' Then the man who had received the one talent came. 'Master,' he said, 'I was afraid and went out and hid your talent in the ground. See, here is what belongs to you.' His master replied, 'You wicked, lazy servant! Well then, you should have put my money on deposit with the bankers, so that when I returned I would have received it back with interest. Take the talent from him and give it to the one who has the ten talents. For everyone who has will be given more, and he will have an abundance. Whoever does not have, even what he has will be taken from him' " (Matt. 25:14a, 25-26a, 27 NIV).

# 1

# The Foundations of Stewardship

Jesus revealed the foundations of stewardship in Matthew 25:14-29. Notice carefully the words entrusted, his property, his servants, the master. Of course, the man in this parable represents Christ, our Savior and our God. Christ assured us that He will reward those who faithfully manage that which He trusts to them. All of us are interested in being rewarded by Him. Every Christian wants to hear Him say "Well done."

**God owns everything.** The first foundational truth of stewardship is this: God owns everything! God has trusted us with His property. Everything that we have received really belongs to Him! God owns everything!

God owns everything by right of creation. Over 40 times between Genesis and Revelation, the Bible affirms that God is the creator. We establish ownership by recording a deed at the place of public records. God's deed, including the legal description, is recorded in Psalm 24:1-2: "The earth is the Lord's, and everything in it, the world, and all who live in it; for he founded it upon the seas and established it upon the waters" (NIV).

God created this entire planet: its surface, land, water, mines, farms, ranches, wildernesses, silver, gold, gems, minerals, and fuels. He even created the constructed and manufactured wealth, buildings, bridges, houses, automobiles, jewelry.

3

Everything belongs to Him because it is made out of the things of the earth that He created. All structured things of the world, including banks, corporations, governments, schools, and institutions, belong to God. "All who live in it," the people, belong to God. No one has leased or bought the world from God.

Everything rightfully belongs to God because He maintains what He created. God revealed this to Job in a very dynamic way (see Job 38-39). The New Testament declares that "in him all things hold together" (Col. 1:17 NIV). Christ, our Lord and God, holds all things together. Recently astronomers published an astonishing discovery. Theorizing that the universe is held together by bits of matter, they searched for this matter with the most recent telescopes. Most of the matter they expected to find was missing. They were left without an explanation of what holds the universe together. Perhaps they should read this verse!

God is the owner of everything by right of redemption. God not only created it and maintains it, He redeemed it. According to Romans 8:19-23 all creation will eventually be liberated from its slavery through the finished redemptive work of Christ. Clearly, God owns all who are saved (1 Cor. 6:19-20). Christ bought us out of sin, condemnation, and death by His own death on the cross. Three things happen when you believe in Christ as your redeemer and surrender your life to Him: you become God's child by spiritual birth (1 Pet. 1:3); you become "joint-heirs" with Christ of all that God has (Rom. 8:17 KJV); you belong to Him, secure forever! You take a giant step toward reality and success when you accept the truth that everything belongs to God.

**God has entrusted some of his possessions to us.** The second foundational truth is this: God has entrusted each of us with the management of some of His possessions (Matt. 25:14 NASB). Entrusted is translated from the Greek word, *paradidomi*, "to deliver to one something to keep, use, take care of, manage." Everything you and I have is an entrustment from God, including our body, mental capacity, soul, relationships, talents, time, positions, possessions, relationships, environment, salvation, prayer, the church, the Bible, the gospel . . . everything we are and have! The questions that support this are straight from the Bible: "For who makes you different from anyone else? What do you have that you did not receive? And if you did receive it, why do you boast as though you did not?" (1 Cor. 4:7 NIV). God cautioned the Israelites about the peril of forgetting this (Deut. 8:11-20).

Entrusted means "made responsible for." Responsibility is a valuable key to experiencing a positive sense of worth and success in life. The Bible word for this is stewardship. A steward is a manager of goods that belong to someone else. For example, the bank where you have an account is a steward of your money.

Our stewardship responsibility is to manage properly everything God has entrusted to us. Proper management means we never forget to Whom it belongs. It also means we have joint participation with God in using His goods to meet needs. Those needs include your own and those of your family, your church, your community, and the world. Stewardship makes you one of God's instruments of blessing to this world.

Stewardship is an expression of a special relationship with God. We are His stewards. What a compliment and a blessing that is. Think of it, God trusts you! In this relationship God grants us two great opportunities. First, He gives us opportunity to prosper (Matt. 25:20-21). God declared through Jeremiah: " 'For I know the plans I have for you,' declares the Lord, 'plans to prosper you and not to harm you, plans to give you hope and a future' " (Jer. 29:11 NIV).

Part of that prosperity is deliverance from the enslavement of greed and me-centered living. God gives you opportunity to prosper in your special entrustment. For example, Noah was entrusted with the responsibilities of building an ark and of saving his family and the animals. Samson was entrusted with strength to deliver Israel from its enemies. Your prosperity may be in imparting education to students, thus preparing them for a better life. Your prosperity may be your children. Every Christian's prosperity includes witnessing about our knowledge of Christ, helping others to experience His salvation, and helping them to grow spiritually.

The second opportunity God gives us is the preparation for a royal eternity. You, if you have accepted Him as your Savior, are destined to be the nobility of eternity (Rev. 22:5)! Just as the children of earthly nobility are trained from infancy, so you are being trained. You are learning the courtesies of the court of heaven. You are learning how to handle freedom and authority. You are learning how to handle responsibility. Stewardship is God's way of training us for reigning with Christ!

**God holds us accountable.** There is a third foundational truth: God holds us accountable for all He has entrusted to us. Accountability, like responsibility, is essential to a healthy life and prosperity. Being accountable motivates us to excellence.

When Christ returns He will settle accounts with us (Matt. 25:19 NIV). Even if His return is "after a long time" and we have passed through death into His presence, the day for settling accounts will come. "For we must all appear before the judgment seat of Christ, that each one may receive what is due to him for the things done while in the body, whether good or bad" (2 Cor. 5:10 NIV). The Christ who gave up His life for you will ask you what you did for Him. We will give account to the Christ who told this story so we would know the day is coming.

Bad stewardship is bad news! The absence of any effort to be a good steward suggests serious shortcomings. Jesus described the scene for us in Matthew 25:24-30. Those who reject stewardship display in three ways the absence of a saving relationship with Jesus Christ. First, they blame their failure on Christ, accusing Him of being hard and unfairly taking from them what He has no right to take (verse 24). Second, they are not even honest with Christ. If they had truly feared Him they would have been motivated to make some effort at stewardship. Finally, Jesus accurately identified them as being wicked, lazy, and worthless (vv. 26, 30). Their faith in and loyalty to Christ is woefully lacking. They have no worth in them. Since every true child of God has worth, the indication is that they are not saved.

God pays faithful stewards well. In this life, they have a sense of purpose and accomplishment. Their resources meet their needs and enable them to help meet the needs of others. They develop good relationships. They enjoy a better mind and a healthier body than those who are not good stewards. They are blessed, and they are a blessing to others. And at the end of life they realize royal status that will last forever (Rev. 22:5), and they will receive a kingdom (Matt. 25:34).

Your faithfulness determines your status! This life is the training ground. Let us vigorously participate!

**Reflections . . .**

1. In two or three paragraphs, describe the impact on you of the fact that God has trusted you with His valuable treasures.

2. Recall at least three biblical examples of God's trust in people; describe how they handled that trust.

3. Make a list of "God's property" (Matt. 25:1) that has been entrusted to you.

4. When you are asked to give account to Him of how you managed His trust, what will you say?

*Therefore, I urge you, brothers, in view of God's mercy, to offer your bodies as living sacrifices, holy and pleasing to God—this is your spiritual act of worship. Do not conform any longer to the pattern of this world, but be transformed by the renewing of your mind. Then you will be able to test and approve what God's will is—his good, pleasing and perfect will" (Rom. 12:1-2 NIV).*

*"Do you not know that your body is a temple of the Holy Spirit, who is in you, whom you have received from God? You are not your own; you were bought at a price. Therefore honor God with your body" (1 Cor. 6:19-20 NIV).*

*"Now we know that if the earthly tent we live in is destroyed, we have a building from God, an eternal house in heaven, not built by human hands. For while we are in this tent, we groan and are burdened, because we do not wish to be unclothed but to be clothed with our heavenly dwelling, so that what is mortal may be swallowed up by life" (2 Cor. 5:1,4 NIV).*

# 2

# Trusted with a Body

Have you ever wondered why God gave you a body, especially the body you have? Probably you will never know all of the reasons, but one fact is obvious. Your body helps you experience life in this world. Think of all the joys you would have missed if God had not given you a body. You would have missed the taste of delicious food, the beauty of a sunset, the comfort of a hug, and a thousand other pleasures. Admittedly, you would also have missed the pains that the body suffers, but even pain has benefits. Evidently God gave you the body you received for good reasons.

Since our bodies are so present with us and so important to us, stewardship of our bodies must be important, too. Stewardship requires that we accept our body as a gift from God; realize how vulnerable our body is; present our body to God as a living sacrifice; develop good bodily communication skills with the world around us; manage our body with moral integrity; glorify God with our body. We want to be ready to give account to God for what we did with our body when we stand before Him.

**Your body is a gift from God. Accept it!** The psalmist wrote, "For you created my inmost being; you knit me together in my mother's womb" (Psalms 139:13 NIV). Do you share his gratitude? A good place to begin good stewardship of your body is by thanking God for it. Although the body is faulty, it is an incredible

creation designed to serve you well. It has a brain for thinking, feet
for walking, hands for working, eyes for seeing, ears for hearing,
a mouth for eating and speaking, a digestive system to secure energy and a circulation system to deliver that energy where your
body needs it, a glandular system to inject the proper chemicals at
the right time, a heart for pumping blood, a liver for purifying the
blood, and an immune system for fighting disease. To top it off,
most of the body functions automatically!

It is fitting to recognize good qualities in a gift we receive from
others. So, it is proper to recognize the positive things about the
body God gave you. Why spend so much time and energy on the
imperfections of your body? Why not make a list of the positive
features of your body and thank God for each one? You may feel
a bit self-conscious at first, but keep in mind you are not compli-
menting yourself, but God, the maker of your body. Include in
your list the characteristics that distinguish you as unique from bil-
lions of other bodies in the world. Your body is an original design
by God. If you are honest, your list will be quite long, a feeling of
gratitude will well up in your heart, and your voice will break out
in praise to your heavenly Father.

While you are working on thankfulness, also list those qualities
of your body that are not so beautiful. Paul mentions them as an
illustration of the church (1 Cor. 12:22-26). All of us have beautiful parts and ugly parts. Have you ever seen a beautiful thyroid
gland? Do you want your lungs on display because they are so
pretty? Yet what would you do without these and other "un-
sightly" parts? They are necessary, and they are some of your
richest assets (2 Cor. 12:7-10).

**Your body is a tent. Realize it!** The human body is called a tent in
the Bible (2 Cor. 5:1,4). One man calls it an "earth suit." Whatever
you call it, your body is a fragile dwelling place. Its usefulness can
be curtailed by disease or accident, and it will eventually die.
Therefore, good stewardship calls for taking care of your body by
eating properly, exercising, and avoiding recklessness.

To be comfortable in a tent you must take care of it. If you let the
floor get wet, you will not sleep well. If you carry food inside, the
bears may come in. Storing it without drying it will cause it to mildew.
If you tear it, your protection is violated. Take good care of your tent!

However, there are limits to how much money and energy
should be spent on a tent. A tent is not pitched to be admired,

but to be used. You can give the quest for a perfect body a higher priority than good stewardship warrants. The use of your body is the real key to good stewardship. Disease and disabilities are not our worst enemy. Sin, our worst enemy, includes both the sins of omission and commission (Matt. 10:28; Rom. 1:24; 6:12).

Our primary effort . . . more important than diet and exercise . . . must be directed toward righteous use of our bodies. You will find that the best regimen for righteousness is seeking to glorify God (1 Cor. 6:20). Joni Earekson Tada has used her imperfect quadriplegic body to bless thousands of people through writing, speaking, and art. On the other hand, we hear news stories of star athletes with "perfect" bodies whose lives have been destroyed because they used their bodies for unrighteous, dishonorable, and detrimental activities.

A good steward will take the best care of his "tent" as possible, for optimum usefulness; concentrate on glorifying God with his body; not lose heart when disease and pain show up without invitation, but continue to play the game even when feeling pain; find cheer in the assurance that the afflictions of this life add to our eternal reward (2 Cor. 4:16-18); come to terms with the "tent," accept it, and make the best of it rather than waste precious time wishing for a better one; through faith in Christ, be prepared for death that often comes as a surprise.

**Your body is a temple. Present it to God!** We live in a time when many worship the temple itself, giving the body inordinate attention. Many people dress it, groom it, pamper it, exercise it, and indulge it like a god, or they deprive it and starve it. Both approaches are overkill. These folks think their body belongs to them, and they can do whatever they please with it. It does not occur to them to acknowledge that Christ bought them with His death on the cross. The idea of turning control of their body over to the Holy Spirit and glorifying God with it is not appealing. Consequently, they rush through life missing the whole point of having a body. Physical and materialistic concerns regarding their bodies come between them and their acceptance of Christ as Savior. The result: their "whole body [will] be thrown into hell" (Matt. 5:29*b* NIV). Jesus commanded us to avoid giving our bodies top priority. Our main concern is seeking His rule and His righteousness (Luke 12:22-31).

Stewardship of the body begins by presenting it to God as a living sacrifice (Rom. 12:1-2). This should be your first decision after receiving Christ as your Savior. The backdrop of that verse is the Old Testament worship that consisted largely of offering sacrifices to God. People in Old Testament times presented to God their best lamb, ram, or bullock. They killed their prized possession and offered it dead on the altar. You have a better offering than them. You have the glorious privilege of presenting your own body, not as a dead offering laying on the altar, but as an offering that lives on. Everywhere it goes and everything it does can be an offering to God. Can you think of a more noble purpose for your body?

There is one other similarity between your presentation of your body and the Old Testament worshipper. When he laid his prize animal on the altar, it never belonged to him again. The New Testament says "you are not your own" (1 Cor. 6:19). You and your body belong to God, to be used by Him as He wills. His spirit is to occupy and control it. You will never again call it your own. You will never again assert your right to do with it as you please. Only His will is to be done with your body! Every day, in every circumstance, wherever you are, you will serve God as though He was incarnate in your body. In your marriage and family relationships your body will honor God. At work, at recreation, on vacation, at church, at every moment, God will have control. You will take into your body only what honors God. You will exercise and rest your body to the glory of God.

Romans 12:1 is addressed to saved people. The presentation does not automatically happen when you are saved. It is your choice; you and you alone can make the presentation. Your parents cannot do it for you at a christening, dedication, or any other time. It could be, and probably should be, done in the privacy of your prayer closet. If, however, the Holy Spirit calls for public commitment, do it.

You present your body to God as a holy sacrifice that is "pleasing to God" (Rom. 12:1*a* NIV). Holy means set apart for God. It is a holy thing to worship and praise God and to study His Word. It is just as holy to present your body to Him. Holy does not eliminate the functions of work, eating, sex with your marriage partner, recreation, or any other proper body function. The Bible clearly presents all of those activities as "pleasing to God" when done according to His commands.

Holy is both negative and positive. Negatively, you are not to use your body like the unsaved use their bodies, for sinful and debauching activities. Positively, you are to use your body in obedience to God's will as revealed in Scripture and applied by His Spirit.

God will accept your offering as your "spiritual service of worship" (Rom. 12:1 NASB). He will accept it if it is fat or thin, tall or short, young or old, healthy or unhealthy. Worship is experiencing the presence of God, adoring Him, and bowing before Him in submission. We frequently limit worship to a church experience. God wants us to experience Him in all of the activities of daily life! Presenting your body to God turns all of life into a worship service.

The God who occupies the temple of your body is the Holy Spirit (1 Cor. 6:19). Even in paganism, a god is in charge of his temple and has free and unrestricted access, and the glory of a temple is the presence of its god. The Holy Spirit began to occupy the temple of your body when you accepted Christ as your Savior. He will be in charge of the temple when you present it to Him. Three questions are necessary. Does the Holy Spirit dwell in your body with free and unrestricted access? Have you presented your body to God as a living sacrifice? If not, when will you?

**Your body is a valuable communication instrument. Use it wisely!** Your body enables you to relate to the world and people around you! You can see, hear, touch, gesture with your hands, nod your head, taste, smell, and speak.

Stewardship involves choosing the kind and quality of your communications. You can use your tongue to praise God and tell the good news of Christ or you can blaspheme God and curse others (James 3:2-12). You can use your sexuality as a blessing to your marriage partner or for debauching promiscuity outside marriage. You can use your hands to earn an honest living and serve humanity, or to abuse others. Your eyes and ears can feed your mind with constructive information or with garbage. Wise stewardship is making good choices.

Parents find their bodies are essential to healthy communication with their children. A parent's physical presence expresses security and love to the children. The face of each parent reflects heartfelt emotions that children recognize when they are quite young. Holding your child's hand while crossing a busy street communicates care and security. Holding a child on your lap can develop your child's sense of worth. Reading to your child will develop thinking skills, an appreciation for reading, and a readiness for successful educational pursuits. Just changing your baby's diaper promptly lays the foundation for faith in God because it teaches your baby that someone out there responds to his cry for help. With your body you can serve a meal, write a check, make a bed, drive your little girl to school, make a dress, and do a thousand other things that express love. Your children will rise up and bless you like the children of the virtuous woman of Proverbs 31:10-31.

**Your body has the awesome power to make another human being. Respect it!** We are stewards of our sexuality: God made us sexual creatures, and He has much to say in His Word about sexual conduct. Stewardship of sexuality includes: accepting your sexual makeup; exercising disciplined control over sexual urges and temptations; remaining a virgin until marriage; refusing to allow abnormal sexual activity to develop; remaining sexually true to your marriage partner (physically and emotionally); meeting the sexual needs of your marriage partner (1 Cor. 7:3-5); dealing with pregnancy and related subjects.

By God's grace, for our emotional, physical, and spiritual health, we to are to accept the sexual nature God gave us. God makes only male or female. Our sinful nature may cause some to be confused at this point. Remember, sin means "to miss the target." In terms of sexuality, the target is either male or female, according to physical makeup. The jury is still out on whether the genes play a role in sexual orientation. Whatever the final verdict, the Bible clearly tells us we all inherit a sinful nature (Psalm 51:5; John 3:6; Rom. 5:12) with sin through our soul, mind, spirit, and body! That sin fault line, with which we are born, causes moral confusion of one kind or another in every human being. Some are confused about their sexual nature, others have confusion over the right and wrong of lying, stealing, or another moral issue. Christ came to save us all from our sins (Matt. 1:21). Everyone, through Christ, must deal with the temptation to perversion. Accepting your sexual nature may be easier for some people than for others. The starting place is recognition of the physical construction of your body, male or female. Christ can help you develop proper acceptance from there.

God designed sexual activity for marriage. It is our means of producing children. It is also an important means of expressing intimacy between husband and wife. It is to be the most private, intimate experience of marriage. Any sexual expression, physical or emotional, outside that intimacy does serious damage to the marriage and to all persons involved. Take note that Jesus clearly taught that adultery can be committed emotionally without any physical contact (Matt. 5:27). This sin of looking lustfully finds wide acceptance in our society, but is a violation of good sexual stewardship. Therefore, men are responsible for how they look at women other than their wives (Matt. 5:27-28), and women are responsible for dressing modestly (1 Tim. 2:9).

Never allow your body to become your master. Keep your body in its place, sexually and every other way! The Apostle Paul wrote that just as athletes discipline their bodies for winning, Christians must discipline their bodies for winning the spiritual prize. If you indulge the desires of your flesh (Eph. 2:3), those desires will take charge of you and make you their slave.

Abortion is one of the big issues of our day; therefore, how can we leave the subject of sexuality without recognizing the stewardship involved in pregnancy? Today's woman frequently hears that she has a right to do with her body what she pleases. In a sense that is true; God has even granted us the right to choose sin. He has also made it clear that we are accountable for our choices, and we will live with the consequences. Good stewardship takes the view that we are free to do with our body only what fits the design and intent of the One Who made us.

Each person voluntarily chooses their sexual activity. Part of a Christian's stewardship of sex is the choice to remain a virgin until marriage and then be absolutely, 100 percent, loyal to that marriage relationship. The laws of our country grant people the right to engage in sexual activity outside marriage. But those laws do not exempt people from living with the consequences. If a pregnancy occurs, the expectant mother has consequences to live with. An abortion alters the consequences, but does not eliminate them. She has her conscience and memory to live with. All of us are responsible to God for all that we do. The best stewardship is abstinence from sex except in marriage; a strong faith that trusts the leadership and providence of God to control conception; acceptance of unexpected pregnancy as a gift from God (Psalm 127:3).

**Your body is a trust from God. Glorify Him with it!** The specific statement is: "Do you not know that your body is a temple of the Holy Spirit, who is in you, whom you have received from God? You are not your own; you were bought at a price. Therefore honor God with your body" (1 Cor. 6:19-20 NIV).

There are infinite ways to glorify God with your body. Some athletes have used their trained body as a platform for witnessing. Esther may have been the first to use her beauty to meet the needs of others, but she was not the last. God used Samson's strong body and Lazarus' sick body to glorify Him. Lazarus became ill and died "for the glory of God" (John 11:4). His death provided Jesus the opportunity to raise him from the dead. His Resurrection caused many to believe in Jesus Christ as their Savior! Even in sickness you can glorify God in your body. We know that God can even use an old body because He used Moses' body after it was 80 years old (Ex. 7:7). God will help common people like you and me to glorify Him with the body He has given us, if we are willing.

God took a human body so He could touch and heal people, talk with them, and offer Himself on the cross as the redeeming sacrifice for our sins (Heb. 10:5-10). A study of how Jesus used His body will give you a good idea of how to be a good steward of your body.

Paul challenges us with his testimony: "According to my earnest expectation and my hope, that . . . Christ shall be magnified in my body, whether it be by life, or by death" (Phil. 1:20 KJV).

Your body is the temple of the Holy Spirit (1 Cor. 6:19); a temple is a place where a priest serves God. You minister as a priest wherever your body is. Christian priests have two basic ministries. One is "offering spiritual sacrifices acceptable to God through Jesus Christ" (1 Pet. 2:5 NIV). Spiritual sacrifices include prayers for your family, your friends, the unsaved where you work, your neighbors, etc., giving (Phil. 4:18), and praising God (Heb. 13:15). The other priestly ministry is to "declare the praises of him who has called you out of darkness into his wonderful light" (1 Pet. 2:9 NIV).

**We are accountable to God for what we do with our body.**
The clear statement of Scripture is: "For we must all appear before the judgment seat of Christ, that each one may receive what is due to him for the things done while in the body, whether good or bad" (2 Cor. 5:10 NIV).

Jesus gave us the best example of being accountable for the use of our bodies. Consider these facts:
• Jesus accepted His physical body, though it must have felt terribly confining and limiting. Think of it, the Lord of glory,

confined to the body of a helpless infant, limited to normal growth patterns, and restricted in time and space by a body. He accepted it as the gift and will of His Father (Heb 10:5-7).

- Jesus fulfilled life in that body, submitted to death in His body, and trusted God to raise it from the dead.
- Jesus overcame the temptations that appealed to His bodily cravings (Matt. 4:2-4). The use of His body to do the Father's will included the Crucifixion.
- Jesus used His body to communicate with us. That was the purpose of His incarnation. Even the trials and sufferings He experienced made Him an understanding High Priest for all believers (Heb. 4:14-16).
- Jesus glorified His Father with His body in His life, death, and Resurrection. He was never selfish with it. He used it freely, as the Father directed, to minister to the needs of people.

Despite how well you care for your body . . . even if you are an excellent steward of your body . . . it is subject to disease and malfunction. It is destined for death and the grave (Heb. 9:27). But we who are saved anticipate a new body at the resurrection (1 Cor. 15:50-58). It will be like Christ's body (Phil. 3:21; 1 John 3:1-3).

In the parable of the talents (Matt. 25:14-30), the one who received five talents managed them well and gained five more. He was commended for that stewardship (Matt. 25:16, 20-21). Proper stewardship of your body will bear compound interest, and you will receive additional blessings and rewards.

### Reflections . . .

1. Have you completely accepted the body that God gave you? If not, take the time to accept it now.
2. Write your own personal plan for being a good steward of your body "tent."
3. If you have not already done so, take the time now to present your body to God as a living sacrifice and as a temple to be occupied by His Spirit.
4. List ways your body glorifies God; ask God to open your understanding.

*J*esus replied: 'Love the Lord your God with all your heart and with all your soul and with all your mind.' This is the first and greatest commandment" (Matt. 22:37-38 NIV).

"Those who live according to the sinful nature have their minds set on what that nature desires; but those who live in accordance with the Spirit have their minds set on what the Spirit desires. The mind of sinful man is death, but the mind controlled by the Spirit is life and peace; the sinful mind is hostile to God. It does not submit to God's law, nor can it do so" (Rom. 8:5-7 NIV).

"Do not conform any longer to the pattern of this world, but be transformed by the renewing of your mind. Then you will be able to test and approve what God's will is—his good, pleasing and perfect will" (Rom. 12:2 NIV).

"Wherefore gird up the loins of your mind, be sober, and hope to the end for the grace that is to be brought unto you at the revelation of Jesus Christ" (1 Peter 1:13 KJV).

"Let this mind be in you, which was also in Christ Jesus: who, being in the form of God, thought it not robbery to be equal with God: but made himself of no reputation, and took upon him the form of a servant, and was made in the likeness of men: and being found in fashion as a man, he humbled himself, and became obedient unto death, even the death of the cross. Wherefore God also hath highly exalted him, and given him a name which is above every name" (Phil. 2:5-9 KJV).

# 3

# Trusted with a Mind

These are times when much emphasis is placed on the mind. IQ levels are rated. Psychologists are important. "Gifted" students receive special care. Information is increasing at explosive rates. Alzheimer's, the dreaded disease that affects memory, haunts us. People even demand a God that conforms to their mental limits.

In contradiction to this, there is an epidemic of mental sluggishness. Teachers report that the average student has little interest in learning. This bent to mental laziness became obvious as I counseled with Mike about problems in his marriage. He complained that his wife was not romantically responsive. When it became evident that Mike didn't understand his wife's emotional needs, I suggested he read a certain book on the subject. He replied that he was not interested in reading a book, but in a few quick suggestions on how to change his wife. Would it surprise you if I told you that Mike has a master's degree and is a schoolteacher?

The mind has great spiritual significance. For example, the greatest commandment of all, according to Jesus, involves the mind. He said, "Love the Lord your God with all your heart and with all your soul and with all your **mind**" (Matt. 22:37 NIV). Added importance springs from the fact that "the renewing of your mind" is how you are transformed from conformity to the world (Rom. 12:2 NIV).

Because the primary battleground with Satan is our mind, it is puzzling that today's brand of Christianity expresses little interest in the mind. The focus is on feeling good. We assign our heart to God and our mind to circumstance and chance. We seem to believe that we were handed this lame mind and can do nothing about it. Why do we take such a fatalistic view of our mental condition?

The mind, according to the Bible, is a rich, pliable gift. Several Hebrew and Greek words are translated "mind." Biblical definitions include: faculties of perceiving, understanding, thinking, feeling, judging, desiring, meditating, imagining, and remembering. To that list the Bible adds the inner man, the will, and the heart. Then the Bible expands into mental conditions or mind-sets such as like-minded, sober-minded, sound-minded, ready-minded, double-minded, and humble-minded.

**We are born with a natural mind.** We begin our life with this natural mind (Rom. 8:6-7) and early in life begin to develop our own unique version of this natural mind. Through the years we develop a complicated mental program to handle all information received and stored. We use that program to reason, solve problems, make plans, worry, imagine, make decisions, develop attitudes, act, and react. We use that program to decide what appetites to satisfy (Eph. 2:3), what emotions to feel, and to determine our priorities and values.

Every experience of life is stored in our natural mind. Some information was deposited without our consent. Other information is there because we chose to watch, listen, read, or experience something. The good steward carefully screens what the mind is exposed to. Frequently people discussing a current movie say, "It's a good movie, except for a few scenes." Take note: the "unwanted" scenes were stored with the "good" scenes in their memory.

The natural mind is seriously flawed by sin (Rom. 1:28) and with desires that are sinful (Eph. 2:3). A study of Romans 8:5-8 gives us valuable insight into the eternally serious problems of the natural mind. The natural mind is set on the things of the flesh, the New Testament word for our unregenerated nature with which we were born. The flesh is interested in physical needs such as food, drink, sex, and shelter; safety and security needs such as locked doors and savings in the bank; social needs, love, acceptance; esteem needs, recognition, or fame; and fulfillment. All of these needs have been perverted and corrupted by sin. Therefore, the works of the flesh fall into the following categories: "sexual immorality, impurity and debauchery; idolatry and witchcraft; hatred, discord, jealousy, fits of rage, selfish ambition, dissensions, factions and envy; drunkenness, orgies, and the like" (Gal. 5:19b-21a NIV). This is why Romans 8:6 says "the mind set on the flesh is death" (NASB).

Also, "The mind set on the flesh is hostile toward God" (Rom. 8:7a NASB). This explains why they crucified Christ and why Saul of Tarsus was persecuting Christians before Christ saved him. It also explains why, one afternoon as I was telling a man about how much God loved him, he rose up in a rage as if he wanted to attack me. His fleshly mind was hostile toward God.

The mind set on the flesh "does not subject itself to the law of God" (Rom. 8:7b NASB). While giving lip service to the law and commands of God, it will not obey them. In fact, the flesh cannot obey God's law. The mind set on the flesh is the mind of the unsaved, unregenerated person who has never received Jesus Christ as personal Savior. Therefore, "those who are in the flesh cannot please God" (Rom. 8:8 NASB). It is not that God is so hard to please. The word cannot means "no power." The flesh has no power to do what pleases God, even if it wanted to.

The natural mind is not capable of understanding the things of the Spirit of God (1 Cor. 2:14) and is blinded to the gospel of Christ (2 Cor. 4:3-4). That mind does not have faith in God and is prone to worry and anxiety (Matt. 6:32). Its imaginations are "futile" (Rom. 1:21). A futile imagination caused the rich fool to think his wealth would satisfy the needs of his soul (Luke 12:16-21).

The natural mind uses flawed and inferior problem-solving skills. It often blames others for our problems. We seem to think that blaming others solves our problem. Many people waste a lifetime blaming their abusive parents, or some other abuser, for their problems. Yes, abusive parents do cause children to have low self-esteem, but blaming them does not raise the self-esteem. Progress is possible only if we take responsibility for the choices we made in reaction to the abuse. Taking responsibility must be followed quickly with a decision to move forward under the Lordship of Christ in the power He supplies.

**Christians receive a spiritual mind.** The spiritual mind is a new mind that becomes ours through the regeneration that God works when we turn from sin and trust Christ as our personal Savior. Its newness is primarily quality. Newness in time is incidental.

The new spiritual mind is set on "the things of the Spirit" (Rom. 8:5*b* NASB). A new capacity for spiritual understanding becomes ours at spiritual birth when the Holy Spirit begins His unending indwelling (John 14:17). He resides in us to teach us all things and guide us into all truth (John 14:25-26; 16:13). The Holy Spirit motivates us to seek spiritual and eternal values.

Through renewing of the mind, saved people are transformed from conformity to this world (Rom. 12:2). I fear that many Christians have overlooked this. They do not know this transforming secret. They are trying to shed their conformity to this world through their own will power and effort while still operating out of the old fleshly mind-set. Isn't it strange that we seem to think of salvation as applying only to our hearts and souls? We assume that our mind needs very little changing, when in fact every aspect of it needs changing. Failure to pursue the renewing of our mind causes us to slip back into old feelings and old ways of thinking. Our old mind was not erased; the old tapes will still play. Unhealthy mental conditions spawned in our unsaved life will demand control. We learn from the Apostle Peter that a saved person can operate out of the fleshly mind. At one point he fell back into thinking the old way. Jesus rebuked him because he savored not "the things that be of God, but those that be of men" (Matt. 16:23*b* KJV). Savor means to "think and understand." Even after the great day of Pentecost He reverted to fleshly thinking (Gal. 2:11-14).

To allow the natural mind to dominate us after we are saved will cause spiritual shipwreck. If we make no effort to nurture and develop the spiritual mind, the natural mind will continue to feed itself on what is available. There is plenty of mental junk food available. The commercials and entertainment on TV appeal to the natural mind. It is natural for us to desire the products that promise happiness, satisfaction, youth, and beauty. It is also natural for us to develop guilt and low self-esteem because we cannot purchase all of those products. We are often tempted as we see sin portrayed as being so enjoyable. The dominate mind-set of our society is the natural mind. Even some religions appeal to the natural mind by presenting rules and rituals as the savior. The

New Age movement, humanism, and religious cults all appeal to the natural mind. They tell us we can successfully become spiritual with our natural mind. Some even suggest that we can change reality with our natural mind. The natural mind travels a dead-end street and will eventually self-destruct.

**Good news! Your mind can be renewed!** I had a new understanding of this truth when a psychiatrist visited me in my office. As she told me about her new faith in Christ, joy radiated from her face. Her testimony was clear and biblical as she expressed her desire to obey her Lord in baptism, church membership, and daily service. With excitement this fully trained, practicing psychiatrist said, "I enjoy Bible study so much because the Bible contains so much mental health."

Every saved person has the capacity to be transformed through the renewing of the mind (Rom. 12:2). Salvation begins with a change of mind (repentance). The Spirit of God awakens our heart to our sinfulness. Our heart calls upon our mind to change. Before that turning we are full of unbelief and bad perceptions, attitudes, thought processes, desires, priorities, values, imaginations, and affections. When we turn from unbelief to faith, God regenerates us and gives a new heart, and begins the process of renewing our mind. Our mind can be reprogrammed. Paul went into the Arabian desert soon after his conversion to get a jump start on this. His ideas of God, Christ, grace, faith, true righteousness, and many other issues were completely changed.

New spiritual thinking can replace old fleshly thinking. Can you, as I can, recall some of the bad stories we listened to and even repeated before we became serious about making Jesus Lord? Those memories seem to surface at such embarrassing times. I wish I could erase those words and stories, but we do not have the power of selective forgetfulness. Someone told me that it is easier to remember than forget. I challenged his statement. He replied, "Memorize a number." I put 436 into my mind. He asked me to repeat the number.

I said, "436."

Then he said, "Now forget it." Of course, I could not forget the number. We cannot exercise selective forgetting, but we can exercise selective recall and choose the material for our meditation. When unwanted thoughts arise we can send them back to their dungeon and replace them with healthy thoughts. The Bible gives us an excellent formula: "Finally, brothers, whatever is true, whatever is noble, whatever is right, whatever is pure, whatever is lovely, whatever is admirable—if anything is excellent or praiseworthy—think about such things" (Phil. 4:8 NIV). This eight-layered screen filters out depressive, destructive, deceptive, demeaning, unjust, impure, love-destroying, embarrassing, inferior, and blaming thoughts!

Please note: the developing of the renewed mind is a lifelong process. Jesus promised believers that "the Holy Spirit, whom the Father will send in my name, will teach you all things and will remind you of everything I have said to you" (John 14:26 NIV). As life unfolds, the Holy Spirit will help the saved person develop the thought patterns, or mind-set program, of the renewed mind.

With Christ we can develop a healthy mind-set. The good news from God can replace the bad news stored up in the old mind. Mary, the mother of Jesus, is a good example. After the shepherds reported to her the things the angel and the heavenly host told them about Jesus, she "pondered them in her heart" (Luke 2:19 NIV). That word pondered means "to bring together in one's mind, confer with oneself." She brought the good news from the shepherds and her other thoughts together and let it rearrange her old thinking.

The Bible also affirms that the saved person can have a sound mind. When Jesus finished with the man of Gadara, the citizens of the country observed him "sitting there, dressed and in his right mind" (Mark 5:15 NIV). We are also assured that "God hath not given us the spirit of fear; but of power, and of love, and of a sound mind (2 Tim. 1:7 KJV). A sound mind includes self-control. With His help we can gain control of our thoughts.

In Christ we can have a growing mind. We begin with very little knowledge. Information is added to information, decisions are added to decisions, feelings are added to feelings, and a network develops. That is true of our natural mind, and it is true of our spiritual mind. It is a sad thing to find a spiritually retarded Christian. Spiritual retardation is the product of poor stewardship.

Believe it! You can be transformed through the renewing of your mind (Rom. 12:2). You are not locked into the old thought patterns, no matter how long they have been there or how deep their ruts.

**God assigns us responsibility for our minds.** " 'Love the Lord your God with all your heart and with all your soul and with all your mind.' This is the first and greatest commandment" (Matt. 22:37-38 NIV). The relative measure of your IQ is not the issue here. "All of the mind you have" is the issue. Entertain only thoughts that are compatible with love for God. Don't forget that God's love is both tender and tough. Feed your mind on every suggestion of God's love for you, His faithfulness to you, His wise and compassionate dealings with you. Read about it in the Bible; make it the meditation into which your idle mind naturally slips; sing about it quietly in your heart. Spend time in meditation, prayer, and thanksgiving at the cross where God forever settled that He loves you! Daily thank the Father and thank Christ for His great love for you.

Reject every idea, suggestion, or thought that slanders or doubts God. Satan is a slanderer; his main work is to slander God. He slandered God to Eve in the Garden of Eden, and he cunningly slanders God today. He will present to you a circumstance and then suggest that God has failed, thus tempting you to turn against God. Satan tried it with Job and will try it with you.

Make every mental function obedient to Christ (2 Cor. 10:5). Our instruction is to "demolish arguments and every pretension that sets itself up against the knowledge of God, and . . . take captive every thought to make it obedient to Christ" (2 Cor. 10:5 NIV). Demolish all thought patterns, systems of logic, problem-solving techniques that are contrary to the teaching of Christ. Ask Christ to help you develop His way of reasoning and solving problems.

Take captive the unresolved problems of the past that are holding you captive, by dealing with them as Jesus instructed. Seek reconciliation with confrontation, confession, apology, and love. Peter is a good example for this. One night, as Peter was thinking with the old mind, he denied he even knew Christ. Fortunately God used Peter's memory to motivate him to deal with that sin. We read that "immediately the cock crowed" and Peter remembered that Jesus had warned him this would happen. Peter "broke down and wept" (Mark 14:72*b* NIV). He could easily have concluded he was a hopeless failure and remained in a guilt-ridden condition for the rest of his life. He could have blamed others, circumstances, even Jesus. He chose to admit his wrong, take responsibility for his actions, and turn back to Christ. In dealing with his past Peter found forgiveness and hope for a great future! With the help of Christ, take your emotions captive. Ask Him to give you the control He used on His own emotions.

Our stewardship calls for us to study and learn. New spiritual information has to be loaded in. Jesus said: "Take my yoke upon you and learn from me" (Matt. 11:29*a* NIV). Jesus' favorite name for his followers was disciple, which includes the idea of being a student. So, we must learn new thought patterns and problem-solving skills!

We need to learn God's ways in every area of our life. Parents need to study and learn about how to be good parents. Husbands and wives need to study and learn how to develop a good marriage. Every Christian needs to study and learn how to be a better witness. All teachers and leaders in the church need to study and learn how to do their work more effectively. We all need to learn how to successfully handle the changes and surprises of life.

Jesus instructed us not to be anxious and worry over the needs of life. He assured us that our Father in heaven will take care of all our needs if we give attention to seeking His kingdom and His will (Matt. 6:25-33). Jesus conducted His life by faith in God's Word and the power of the Holy Spirit. Recall how He slept calmly in the boat on the stormy sea. Without the aid of drugs, you can experience that same tranquility. "Do not be anxious about anything, but in everything, by prayer and petition, with thanksgiving, present your requests to God. And the peace of God, which transcends all understanding, will guard your hearts and your minds in Christ Jesus" (Phil. 4:6-7 NIV).

Meditation, a strong, healthy mental process, was not invented by the Eastern religions. It is as old as the book of Genesis (Gen. 24:63). We all meditate: some call it worry; some call it daydreaming; some call it deep thought or other names. Meditation on the wrong material can lead to destruction. On the other hand, the Bible promises great peace and prosperity to those who meditate on God's Word (Psalm 1:2).

"Gird your mind for action" (1 Peter 1:13*a* NASB) is an interesting command. Those New Testament people understood the metaphor. They wore long flowing garments tied around the waist with a girdle (belt). When an emergency came, they would quickly gather up those flowing robes, tying them together with the girdle so they would not be hindered from taking swift action.

Our minds tend to be like those freely flowing robes, twisting around us, hindering us from victoriously handling life. Past abuse trips up our self-worth. Fears lock us in a terrifying prison. Unreconciled relationships cripple joy with bitterness and guilt. Selfish insecurity expressed as jealousy sabotages marriage. Depressive thoughts shackle the mind in a dark room of despair. Doubts keep us from experiencing peace of mind . . . common doubts like "Am I really saved?"; "Is my husband faithful?"; "Is my job secure?"; "Did God really create us?"; "Is the Bible trustworthy?"; "Does God truly exist?"

Good stewardship calls for us to "get together" all of our loose, harmful thought patterns and put them under the control of Christ. Take heart; there is solid hope. You can gird your mind. The Bible affirms that our minds can be renewed (Rom. 12:2). Girding your mind is an essential part of that renewing. This "mind girdle" is woven from seven strong fibers identified in 1 Peter 1:13-25.

1. Sobriety (v. 13). We cannot be good stewards of our minds if we intoxicate them with alcohol or drugs.

2. Hope (v. 13). God has given us hope founded on the Resurrection of Christ and focused on the grace Christ will bring us when He returns. We have never been, nor are we yet, worthy of living forever with the holy God in the perfect heaven. Here is our hope: when Christ comes, He will bring us all the grace we need to fit us for that glory!

3. Desire to be like God in holy conduct (vv. 14-15). Just as a child wants to be like a parent, we are to desire to be like God. We are to stop obeying the former lust of our old sinful nature and, at every temptation, decide to be an obedient child of our Father in heaven. As God is holy, upright in character, maintaining unimpeachable integrity, morally pure in thought and action, we are to be holy in all our behavior.

4. Fear God (v. 17). Do these words trouble you? Some fears are proper. The person who works with high-voltage electricity must have a healthy fear of contacting the wire. Stop and think about it: we conduct much of our lives out of fear. For example, we fear financial ruin so we work; we fear embarrassment so we dress up. However, our fears are off target due to our sinfulness. Though many of our fears are

unfounded and damaging, when we fear God unwarranted
fears fade away and legitimate fears arrange themselves
properly. Moreover, when we fear God, we find we have
nothing to fear! We have nothing to fear from Him Who
loves us enough to die for us. He will never abuse us. We
discover we have nothing to fear from any other source; He
is our shield and deliverer.

5. Remember you were redeemed by the precious blood of
   Christ (vv. 18-19). By paying the supreme price, He de-
   clared us very valuable to God. We are more obligated to
   Him than anyone or anything else.

6. Love the brethren fervently (v. 22). The love named here
   is completely unselfish in its practical care for others. It is
   the word used in John 3:16 to name God's love for us, love
   that moved Him to give His only begotten Son to save us.
   Great refreshing comes to the person who loves like this
   (Isa. 58:3-11).

7. Desire the sincere milk of God's Word (1:23 to 2:2). Our
   desire is to be like that of a newborn baby with a con-
   suming desire for milk. He has no desire for money,
   power, or fame. He does not care what or whom he in-
   terrupts to satisfy that desire. It is top priority on his
   agenda. We should have this same kind of desire to feed
   our minds, hearts, and souls on the Bible so that we may
   grow strong toward maturity!

**Permit God to develop an unselfish mind in you.** We read
"let this mind be in you, which was also in Christ Jesus" (Phil.
2:5 KJV). The word for mind here involves attitude. Jesus gave
up His status of equality with God in order to be our Savior. He
gave up His position as King of Glory and took the lowest of
all positions, a slave. Jesus gave up His control of everything
and became obedient, even obeying those who plotted and car-
ried out His Crucifixion. "He was oppressed and afflicted, yet
he did not open his mouth; he was led like a lamb to the
slaughter, and as a sheep before her shearers is silent, so he did
not open his mouth" (Isa. 53:7 NIV). He did all of this to serve
and save us. Therefore, God has highly exalted Him and His
name above all others. The path to the renewed mind leads
through service. Dark days may come while serving, but the
end of the journey is glory!

Stewardship of the mind begins with salvation. It continues as the saved person pursues the renewing of the mind. That pursuit will call for reading, seeking Christian counsel, listening, self-denial, and making tough choices and changes. The outcome will be transformation!

**Reflections . . .**
1. Review this chapter, underlining characteristics of the natural mind.
2. Identify areas of your mind that need to be renewed.
3. List actions you can take to renew your mind.
4. List the seven fibers of the "girdle" for the renewed mind.

*There are different kinds of gifts, but the same Spirit. There are different kinds of service, but the same Lord. There are different kinds of working, but the same God works all of them in all men. Now to each one the manifestation of the Spirit is given for the common good. To one there is given through the Spirit the message of wisdom, to another the message of knowledge by means of the same Spirit, to another faith by the same Spirit, to another gifts of healing by that one Spirit, to another miraculous powers, to another prophecy, to another distinguishing between spirits, to another speaking in different kinds of tongues, and to still another the interpretation of tongues. All these are the work of one and the same Spirit, and he gives them to each one, just as he determines" (1 Cor. 12:4-11 NIV).*

# 4

# Trusted with an Ability

Do you have a God-given ability that could both help people and glorify Jesus Christ? Before you say no, let me ask you some other questions. Can you walk or talk? Do you have ears and eyes, hands and feet? Is your head bald or covered with hair? You will probably say, "Of course, but those are characteristics we all have in common." Is it possible you are overlooking a vital area of stewardship just because it is so "common"?

**All abilities are gifts of God.** It is written that God "gives all men life and breath and everything else" (Acts 17:25*b* NIV). So the ability to breathe, walk, talk, think, speak, and all other common abilities are gifts of God. Receiving a gift from God makes us a steward of that gift.

Learn from the lad David, son of Jesse. When he volunteered to fight Goliath, King Saul said, "You are not able to go out against this Philistine and fight him; you are only a boy, and he has been a fighting man from his youth" (1 Sam. 17:33 NIV). Notice the word *able*. David responded by telling Saul how he had killed a lion and a bear that attacked the sheep. Then David added: "The Lord who delivered me from the paw of the lion and the paw of the bear will deliver me from the hand of this Philistine" (1 Sam. 17:37 NIV). David gave God the credit for his ability to defeat the lion, the bear, and Goliath.

Later he wrote: "Praise be to the Lord my Rock, who trains my hands for war, my fingers for battle" (Psalm 144:1 NIV). You may think that it would be difficult to honor God with an ability to fight. That is exactly the point. All abilities come from God and can be used to glorify Him. The Bible affirms that King David used His God-given fighting ability to fulfill the purposes of God in liberating many oppressed people.

A few years ago I learned a new appreciation for the gift of walking. A few minutes after breakfast, the room began to spin around and around. For several weeks before, I had experienced some attacks of dizziness that lasted only a few seconds. I thought this was just another attack and would go away soon. I was standing by the kitchen sink, so I leaned against the cabinet and slid to a sitting position on the floor, but the attack did not go away. Even with my eyes closed I felt like I was spinning around. I crawled a few feet to the carpet in the next room and fell flat on the floor.

Three hours later I was no better, so I asked my son to dial 911. The hospital made some tests and diagnosed the problem as an acute case of labyrinthitis, caused by a viral attack on my balance system. About midnight I awoke and realized the spinning had stopped, but when I tried to stand up, I fell. My sense of balance was gone. For two weeks the best I could do was crawl on the floor. The first time I was able to stand for a few minutes I thanked God. I learned that just being able to stand up and walk is a precious gift. The statement of Jesus, "Apart from me you can do nothing" (John 15:5 NIV) had new meaning to me. Every ability is an important gift!

**Everyone has common ability.** The mix is a little different with each one. Even if some common ability such as walking, seeing, or hearing, is missing, you have a host of other abilities. These common abilities equip us for the routines of daily life. When these common abilities are placed in the hands of Christ, daily routines become acts of ministry and service. Cleaning house can become something you do with love for your family, guests, and Christ. Using your ears to listen carefully to others can honor Christ and bless their lives. Remember the little girl, captured from Israel and serving Naaman's wife? When Naaman discovered he was a leper, the girl told the wife of Naaman about the prophet in Israel who could help him. A common girl spoke simple words with a common voice, and a great man's life was changed (2 Kings 5:1-19)!

Any ability, no matter how small, can be used to glorify God and inspire others. It was true in Bible times. A little boy had only a lunch of five loaves and two fish, but in the hands of Jesus they became one of the most talked about miracles of all time (Mark 8:1-8). What was true in Bible times is true today. Lorene was in college when I was. She was a radiant Christian though she used a wheelchair. Traveling from class to class and floor to floor was difficult. Every time I saw Lorene she had a happy smile. None of us ever heard her complain. She had the ability to smile during very trying times. We were all inspired by her. Across the years, when having severe difficulties, I have remembered Lorene's smile and have been inspired to carry on. A common smile may be much more powerful than you think.

There was a woman in my hometown, during my teen years, who was a good cook of common food . . . nothing fancy. She also had a heart to serve Christ by ministering to others. When she heard of someone who needed an emotional lift, she would bake a cake or some cookies and quietly slip it into their house. She would leave a note, "Given in the name of our Blessed Lord." Her cooking never won a prize at the county fair, but it did win many people to Christ because she loved enough to do what she could. She showed us that the New Testament Christianity of Dorcas is still alive. Dorcas glorified Christ and won others to Him with her needle and thread (Acts 9:36-42). Dorcas did not sit and long for some notable talent with which to serve her Lord; she simply made garments for the widows in Joppa. Faithfulness in using her needle to show love made a difference in Joppa. When she suddenly died, Peter was called in to help. He found the widows grieving and testifying of her loving deeds. Through God's power Dorcas was restored to life. The Bible records the results with these words: "This became known all over Joppa, and many people believed in the Lord" (Acts 9:42 NIV). Yes, we are stewards of even the common abilities God has trusted to us.

**Some people have uncommon abilities.** I knew a man who could take a knife and carve an ordinary piece of wood into a work of art. He was not handsome. His clothes sagged in disarray on his shapeless body. There was evidence that his IQ was below average, and he was not very friendly. But he had an unusual talent for carving wood.

When God was instructing Moses how to build the tabernacle He said: "See I have chosen Bezalel . . . and I have filled him with the Spirit of God, with skill, ability and knowledge in all kinds of crafts—to make artistic designs for work in gold, silver and bronze, to cut and set stones, to work in wood, and to engage in all kinds of craftsmanship. Moreover, I have appointed Oholiab . . . to help him. Also I have given skill to all the craftsmen to make everything I have commanded you" (Ex. 31:3-6 NIV). God gave those men uncommon abilities to work with metal, jewels, and other construction materials. Does it seem strange that the filling with the Spirit of God is connected with cutting stones and carving wood? God's Spirit can turn a talent into a ministry! Without God's Spirit, the talent will likely bring honor to the person, but not to God.

Some people today have uncommon abilities. Some can perform surgery, others skillfully practice law, still others excel in sports, or music, or making money. None of these are considered holy activities, but under the control of God's Spirit they become holy. The battle for the souls of men, women, youth, and children is raging in the everyday world. It rages in the entertainment world, the business world, the legal world, the medical world, and every area of daily life. Christ needs soldiers on those battlefields, using their God-given uncommon abilities to minister and witness the truth of God. That's stewardship!

**Hiding or denying an ability is not good.** The man who received one talent buried it in the ground (Matt. 25:24-25). He probably thought it was too small to matter. His grave mistake surfaced when the master came to settle accounts with them. His one talent was taken from him, and he was cast out. Whatever that means, it is not good. Only those who honestly admitted they had received a gift and used it were rewarded.

**Every saved person has at least one body gift.** A "body gift" equips a Christian to render special service as a member of a church. Every saved person has a special ability for serving in a church (1 Cor. 12:7). No saved person is left out. If you have been saved you have a gift. You may not know what it is; you may have never heard of it before; but you have at least one gift.

Saved people do not have the same gifts. Rather, there are many different kinds of gifts. You will find several lists in the Scriptures (Rom. 12:6-9; 1 Cor. 12:8-10, 28; Eph. 4:11). Every church has different needs; every church needs different gifts. All churches need people who smile, are friendly, care for children, write, grow flowers, hoe weeds, run sound systems, clean floors, give money, paint walls, teach, sing, play music, and preach.

Dixie Middleton had a nice car. The church had several members who were widows, advanced in years and not able to drive. Dixie used her car like a taxi to take those widows to the mall or grocery store. They were helped, the church prospered, and Dixie was happy.

Madeline is a retired secretary who loves to write letters. She writes letters to the missionaries, former members, and anyone else who has an interest in the church. Madeline also mails a card to every church member on their birthday. She pays for this ministry herself. She is a blessing to many people. God has gifted you to fulfill His unique purposes for you and for His church.

The Holy Spirit bestows the gifts. They do not come from any human source. They are Holy Spirit given and Holy Spirit empowered. The gifts differ, but the one and same Spirit gives them (1 Cor. 12:11$a$). He is sovereign in bestowing body gifts (1 Cor. 12:11$b$ NIV).

"Now the body is not made up of one part but of many" (1 Cor. 12:14 NIV). Just like the human body has many members, the church has many members. No two members have the same responsibility. They may have similar responsibilities such as teaching, ushering, or singing, but each has a special application of that similar responsibility. I can see and read with just one eye, but the other enhances vision and adds depth perception. If one member of the body decides to stop functioning because its job is not very important, the body is handicapped. Many churches limp along with handicaps because some members are not exercising their gifts.

The gifts are given "for the common good" (1 Cor. 12:7 NIV). Your gift is not given for your selfish enjoyment or use, but to equip you for a unique service in your church. You are to use it for the good of the entire church. For example, when my body says it is hungry, my mind tells my feet to take me to the dinner table, my hands use the fork to put the food in my mouth, my mouth chews the food and sends it to my stomach where digestion begins, and my entire body is strengthened. None of the many members of my body exists for itself alone. So it is in the church body.

The Bible clearly presents the church as the context for using our gifts and talents. Your hands, feet, eyes, and heart work in the context of your body. The body parts must be closely knit together to function. A hand cannot serve the body if it is detached from the body. The parts must work together in harmony to accomplish anything. Also, if the body parts compete and are not coordinated, the body is dysfunctional. When the members of the church apply their gifts in harmony, the body is built up (Eph. 4:16).

**You will be blessed by discovering and using your gifts.** When the apostles returned from Sychar with food they said to Jesus, "Rabbi, eat something" (John 4:31 NIV). Jesus replied, "I have food to eat that you know nothing about" (John 4:32 NIV). They wondered where He got this secret food. "My food," said Jesus, "is to do the will of him who sent me and to finish his work" (John 4:34 NIV). Remember, Jesus had been walking for hours, and it was past mealtime. The woman who came to draw water had just been saved. Jesus was so filled that He lost His physical hunger. His needs were met as He served His Father. That is true for us. When we use our abilities to serve Christ our needs are met! You could call this one of the perks of faithful stewardship.

You are responsible for *only* the gifts you have, but you are responsible for *all* the gifts you have. In the parable of the talents, each person received a different number of talents. Each was responsible for only what he was given.

Discovery of your gift is very important. The Holy Spirit assigns you responsibility when He bestows the gift. Your blessings begin when you discover the gift and begin to exercise it. Both you and God's Spirit have a role in discovering your gifts. Your role includes a thankful attitude and a willingness to use them for God's purpose and glory. The Spirit's role is to reveal to you what you need to know when you need to know it. Be patient; Moses was 80 years old when God revealed His assignment for delivering Israel. A word of caution: carefully avoid envying the talents of another or looking with disdain on the talents God gave you.

Into this quest for understanding, God has put a wonderful dynamic that involves us in fellowship with Him. Prayer is a good place to start. Begin by admitting to yourself and then to God that He has given you at least one ability or gift. Tell Him you believe His Word, and since you know He is no respecter of persons, you believe He gave gifts to you. Thank Him, by faith, for being so gracious to you and for all the gifts you have received, although you do not yet know what they are.

Two common clues to discovering your ability are finding an activity that appeals to your interest and listening to what your fellow Christians say about your gifts. Check out the activities that you enjoy; if this is a gift from God, He will bless your efforts. What do your fellow Christians say about your abilities? They may see an ability before you do.

Discovery of God's gifts can be very rewarding. Most children and many adults are anxious to open their gifts at Christmas. They expect the gift to be wonderful. All gifts of God are wonderful, even those that do not seem wonderful on the surface. I knew a preacher in Texas who had an unusually large head, and it was bald. He told me that at first he was ashamed of his head, but then he realized it distinguished him from others. So he turned this "gift" into a tool for witnessing. He developed a good sense of humor and frequently made jokes about his bald head. God used that humor to help people feel comfortable in his otherwise intimidating presence. His sense of humor opened opportunities for him to witness.

Eagerly seek training to sharpen the use of your ability. Keep in mind that Jesus chose the Twelve and gifted them to be apostles. Then He spent three years training them with such intense activity that at times they had no time to eat their meals. A dull ax is still an ax, but a sharp ax will cut more wood with less effort than a dull ax.

When you discover your gifts and exercise them, three wonderful things begin to happen. The church will be blessed; Christ will be honored; you will be rewarded. These blessings are good evidence you have found your gift.

God gave Paul a "thorn in the flesh" (2 Cor. 12:7 KJV) which Paul wanted taken away. But God revealed to him the thorn was for his good, to keep him humble so the power of Christ would dwell in him. Paul decided to "glory in" and "take pleasure in" the thorn. Whatever the gift(s) are, you are responsible for using them according to His plan.

**Faithfulness in the use of your talents is the key to eternal success.** I remember a man who had served his church faithfully as a deacon, Sunday School director, and music director. As his age increased, younger people were chosen for those notable works. He still had a love for people and a warm way of greeting them. He decided he would help others feel wanted and welcome when they came to worship. It was not a commanding position but, as Jesus said, the one who serves becomes the greatest. When they celebrated Floyd's departure to glory—his funeral—the church house was packed. The pastor, Roy Edgeman, preached from Romans 8, Floyd's favorite passage, and some were saved as a result. Talents may not appear as we think they should. It looked like Floyd's talents were diminishing, but they were actually expanding.

Stewardship of abilities begins with thankful acceptance of the abilities God has given you. It continues with the discovery of what these abilities are and the faithful use of them within your local church body for the purposes of God. In the process, other talents may become yours and your ministry will expand. Stewardship ends in that awesome moment when we stand before Christ, accountable to Him (Luke 16:2).

The wise man wrote: "Whatever your hand finds to do, do it with all your might" (Eccl. 9:10*a* NIV).

**Reflections . . .**

1. Write a brief statement describing your perception of the difference between common and uncommon abilities.

2. No doubt you have written a "thank you" note to a friend for a gift. In a similar way write a "thank-you" note to God for every ability (common and uncommon) He has given you.

3. Write out a plan for putting your "body gifts" into service in your church. Share this with your pastor.

*There is a time for everything, and a season for every activity under heaven: a time to be born and a time to die, a time to plant and a time to uproot, a time to kill and a time to heal, a time to tear down and a time to build, a time to weep and a time to laugh, a time to mourn and a time to dance, a time to scatter stones and a time to gather them, a time to embrace and a time to refrain, a time to search and a time to give up, a time to keep and a time to throw away, a time to tear and a time to mend, a time to be silent and a time to speak, a time to love and a time to hate, a time for war and a time for peace" (Eccl. 3:1-8 NIV).*

*"See then that ye walk circumspectly, not as fools, but as wise, redeeming the time, because the days are evil. Wherefore be ye not unwise, but understanding what the will of the Lord is" (Eph. 5:15-17 KJV).*

*"Trust in the Lord and do good; dwell in the land and enjoy safe pasture. Delight yourself in the Lord and he will give you the desires of your heart. Commit your way to the Lord; trust in him and he will do this: He will make your righteousness shine like the dawn, the justice of your cause like the noonday sun. Be still before the Lord and wait patiently for him; do not fret when men succeed in their ways, when they carry out their wicked schemes" (Psalm 37:3-7 NIV).*

# 5

# Trusted with Time

Are you going somewhere or just traveling? Time is opportunity to "go somewhere" with life. Traveling to the right destination calls for wise stewardship of time. Wisdom in time stewardship includes knowing what time is according to the Bible; redeeming time; understanding the will of God; doing the will of God. "Just traveling" aimlessly through life is not the way to reach the right destination.

**What is time according to the Bible?** The word for time in Ephesians 5:16 suggests a measure of time, or a season, or an opportunity. Most translations prefer the word opportunity, but the Greek word calls for wider application. For example, Mark 10:30 refers to an era and in Matthew 16:3 it is the times in which we live. In Matthew 21:41 the word is translated "seasons." Time is minutes, days, years, a moment of opportunity, the seasons of life, or the exciting times in which we live.

Do we all have the same amount of time? The answer is both yes and no. Yes, if amount means each of us has 60 seconds per minute, 60 minutes per hour, and 24 hours per day. No, if amount means time that is available for our personal control. For example, when a woman chooses to become a mother she changes the amount of time available for her personal use. Also, we do not all live the same number of years. So each of us is allotted a unique amount of seconds, days, months, and years. We are stewards of how we manage our time allotment.

**Redeeming time is our grand stewardship opportunity!**
Redeem means "paying a price to recover from the power of another." Wise use of time is not automatic. We must pay a price, expend effort, set priorities, and make plans to redeem time. Otherwise we become the victim of the clock and the calendar, and the evil times in which we live will set our agenda. To let time slip by unredeemed is to let life slip by unredeemed.

"The days are evil" (Eph. 5:16*b* KJV). Therefore, we must redeem them. Evil means "full of labors, annoyances, hardships, perils, sin, and wrongdoing." All of these characteristics of evil come naturally and automatically in life. The world's agenda is evil. Sinning is featured in our time. Many people simply endure the week so they can have another sin-filled weekend. People entertain themselves with sex, lust, and violence. Merchants use those same vices to sell everything from cars to toys. Greed is corrupting our values. Unresolved hatred and guilt are destroying our peace of mind. Addiction to alcohol, drugs, and work robs us of quality life. Success, by the world's definition, is wealth, position, power, and popularity. Jesus said we are "sheep in the midst of wolves" (Matt. 10:16*a* KJV). If we simply take whatever agenda the times hand us, the result will be evil.

The middle voice of the verb *redeem* suggests that we redeem the time for ourselves. No one else can redeem time for me or for you. Whatever others do, whatever the times call for, whatever others suggest, you must redeem your time from evil and manage it yourself. Other people will set the agenda for you if you do not have an agenda of your own.

There is a promise in the challenge of Ephesians 5:16. It says we can win over the evil; we can change the pattern; we can redeem the opportunity and seize the moment. We can even influence our times toward Christ!

The day will come when we give an account to our Lord for our stewardship of time. The day of judgment has been appointed (Acts 17:31). Wise advice is given us in Romans 13:12-14: "The night is nearly over; the day is almost here. So let us put aside the deeds of darkness and put on the armor of light.

Let us behave decently, as in the daytime, not in orgies and drunkenness, not in sexual immorality and debauchery, not in dissension and jealousy. Rather, clothe yourselves with the Lord Jesus Christ, and do not think about how to gratify the desires of the sinful nature" (NIV).

Establishing good priorities and setting healthy boundaries are essential to good stewardship of time. The Bible speaks of discerning excellent priorities (Phil. 1:10). It is easier to choose inferior priorities than it is to choose excellent priorities.

To choose excellent priorities we must take two basic actions. First, consider what areas of life need priority time, energy, and resources. Include family, church, vocation, personal growth (spiritual, mental, social, and physical). Next, establish the proper balance of time, energy, and resources for each priority. For example, in the area of family, priority should be given to the marriage relationship, relating to each child, and managing the family finances. This establishment of priorities will not be accomplished overnight and must stay fluid as the needs of life change.

It is impossible to establish excellent priorities without the illumination of God. We are too blind or nearsighted and too short of understanding to do it alone. But here is the good news: God is very interested in helping us do this. He will give wisdom to anyone who asks in faith (James 1:5-8). Good use of time will emerge from following good priorities.

**Understanding God's will is essential to proper time management.** Redeeming the time is doing the right thing at the right time, and this is how the Bible focuses on time management. The time management focus of the world is on efficiency. We make lists, budget time, organize, schedule, and plan to keep from wasting a single moment. Time management books and seminars abound and can be helpful to a committed steward. However, you can use time efficiently by the world's standards and still not be doing the right thing. It is possible to climb the ladder to success efficiently, only to discover that it is leaning against the wrong wall. The Bible emphasizes choosing to lean your ladder against the "right" wall. Taking the right action at the right time in pursuit of the right priorities is good time stewardship. The issue is not doing things right, but doing the right things.

Doing the right thing at the right time is possible only if we understand and do the will of God. God alone is wise enough to know what the right thing is. He knows the demands of today and tomorrow. God knows your potential. He knows how to lead you from where you are to where you need to go. God cares; He loves you more than all the others who ask for your time. You can trust Him, the one who gave His only Son to save you, to lead you in the right way and to the right destination.

We do not naturally understand the will of God. In our focal passage in Ephesians 5, there are two interesting word plays on wise and foolish. The first is in verse 15: "Be very careful, then, how you live—not as unwise but as wise" (NIV). Unwise and wise are the negative and positive forms of the same word, *sophia. Sophia* is a rich word meaning "skill, wisdom, and piety." It is used in the Septuagint translation of Psalms 111:10: "The fear of the Lord is the beginning of wisdom." So this wisdom comes from proper respect for God and His will.

The second play on words is in verse 17: "Therefore do not be *foolish*, but *understand* what the Lord's will is" (Eph. 5:17 NIV). Being foolish is set in contrast with understanding what the Lord's will is. This word foolish refers to a person who does not think or weigh issues, or carefully seek God's will before deciding. Understanding God's will calls for thinking, weighing issues, and positively seeking God's will.

Understanding involves more than knowing facts. It is "getting the facts together, comprehending, perceiving." For example, Luke used this Greek word *suneimi* to describe the inability of Mary and Joseph to understand Jesus' actions at age 12 (Luke 2:50). Though Mary and Joseph put the facts together, they still did not understand the actions of Jesus. Just knowing many Scripture passages by memory does not mean you understand their meaning or how to fit them together to properly discern God's will.

The strongest obstacle to understanding God's will is our strong desire to set our own agenda and do our own will. Understanding God's will includes discarding our agenda and wholeheartedly accepting His agenda.

God freely reveals His will in His Word, the Bible. The Ten Commandments clearly state His will. The Sermon on the Mount clearly states His will. Many passages say outright, "This is God's will." For example, we know it is God's will to deliver us from the evil of this present world because the Bible says that Christ "gave himself for our sins to rescue us from the present evil age, according to the will of our God and Father" (Gal. 1:4 NIV). We know that it is God's will for us to work at our job with integrity and dependability because it is stated in Ephesians 6:6.

First Thessalonians 4:3 declares plainly that it is God's will that we abstain from sexual fornication. It is the stated will of God that we give thanks in everything (1 Thess. 5:18). In 1 Peter 2:15 we are told that it is God's will that we be good law-abiding citizens. God's will can even include suffering for doing good, according to 1 Peter 3:17 and 4:19. It is God's revealed will that marriages be strong and fulfilling, and that husbands and wives become one (Eph. 5:21-33). It is God's will that parents fulfill their role effectively and that children honor and obey their parents (Eph. 6:1-4).

It is God's will that parents provide for the material, emotional, physical, and spiritual needs of their children (1 Tim. 5:8). It is God's will that we be honest in all our business dealings and never incur debt beyond our ability to pay (Rom. 13:8). Praying, worshipping, giving, witnessing, and exercising our spiritual gifts are all God's will.

God's purposes for us reveal His will. For example, it is God's purpose that we become like Christ. "For those God foreknew he also predestined to be conformed to the likeness of his Son, that he might be the firstborn among many brothers" (Rom. 8:29 NIV; see also Eph. 4:11-15). Good stewardship of time includes provision for growing into Christlikeness. Christ was a perfect time manager, always doing the right thing at the right time (John 7:6,8). Consider some examples: He was born at the right time (Gal. 4:4); He began preaching at the right time (Mark 1:15); He went to Jerusalem for the Crucifixion at the right time (Luke 9:51); He was betrayed and crucified at the right time (Mark 14:41). Good stewardship of time is pursuing growth into Christlikeness.

God has declared that there is a time for everything. Being *in time* is more important than being *on time*. A sewing machine is a good example of the importance of being *in time*. The working parts of the machine must move precisely *in time* with each other for the seam to be proper. If the machine gets *out of time* the seam will not be right despite the intentions and efforts of the tailor. So, if we are not *in time* with God's will, life will not turn out right, whatever our efforts and intentions.

God's Spirit, who dwells within us, reveals His will to us. Jesus said that the Spirit will guide us into all truth (John 16:13), teach us all things, and remind us of what Jesus said (John 14:26). We also read that the Spirit prays for us "according to the will of God" (Rom. 8:27 KJV). He can guide us to know what the will of God is in any circumstance. The Spirit abides within us to help us do God's will, "for it is God who works in you to will and to act according to his good purpose" (Phil. 2:13 NIV). Knowing this, we can use our time to the maximum efficiency. Paul, the human writer of our focal Scripture (Eph. 5:15-17), conducted his life by the will of God as revealed in the Bible and by the Holy Spirit. His vocational choice as well as the epistles he penned was by the will of God. On his second missionary journey he tried to go to Asia, but the Holy Spirit forbade it. He then tried to go to Bithynia, but the Spirit did not allow it. So he went forward to Troas where God revealed to him that he should go to Macedonia (Acts 16:7-10).

God's will is that we do what He reveals as important, not what others say is urgent. Again, our example is Jesus. He was ministering in Capernaum. People were gathering around Him, seeking Him, listening to Him, and requesting His ministry. It was late that night when the last sick person was healed. Early the next morning, before daylight, Jesus arose from His bed, slipped out of the house, down the street, and out of town to a private place to pray.

When the city awoke, people came to the house for Jesus again. Simon and the disciples searched for Him, and when they found Him they reminded Him, "Everyone is looking for you" (Mark 1:37 NIV). Instead of responding to the urging of the disciples and of the people, Jesus went to a nearby town to minister. He chose to do the important rather than the urgent.

Later, Jesus said to a man, " 'Follow me.' But the man replied, 'Lord, first let me go and bury my father. Jesus said to him, 'Let the dead bury their own dead, but you go and proclaim the kingdom of God' " (Luke 9:59-60 NIV). We must never let what seems urgent to us set our agenda! God's will is the truly urgent action for us to take.

Good stewardship of time begins with understanding and doing the will of God. It touches every area of life . . . home, marriage, sex, parent-child relationships, finances, food, clothing, debt, savings, vocation, recreation, church, and worship.

Good stewardship of time will not bind us up in a stressful schedule! Over involvement is not good stewardship. Rest is an essential part of good time management. God rested and set aside one day each week for rest and worship (Ex. 20:8-11). God put three weeks into the Old Testament calendar for everyone to stop working and celebrate. Every 7th year and every 50th year were to be different in work demands and celebration. God will never "burn us out" with doing His will. He has special refreshment and strength for those who "wait on him" (Isa. 40:31 KJV). Wait means looking to God expectantly, fully assured that doing His will is primary and that God will empower us to do it. God's Spirit is the source of our strength and bears wonderful fruit in us: "love, joy, peace, patience, kindness, goodness, faithfulness, gentleness and self-control" (Gal. 5:22-23 NIV).

**The Bible reminds us to be good time stewards.** Daily reminders are given . . . morning, noon, and evening are times for seeking God in prayer, in meditation, in His Word, and in worship (Psalm 5:3; 55:17; 59:16; 88:13; 119:147; 143:8). Sundown is the deadline for being angry. The sun is not to go down on our wrath or exasperation (Eph. 4:26).

The Bible gives us weekly and seasonal reminders. Sunday, the first day of the week, is the time for gathering with our fellow believers in worship and giving (1 Cor. 16:2). A major purpose for gathering together for worship is to encourage one another and "stimulate one another to love and good deeds" (Heb. 10:23-25 NASB). All of us need encouragement and motivation. We gather to be encouraged and motivated, but we are also there to encourage and stimulate others. This is good stewardship of time.

"Six days shalt thou labour, and do all thy work" (Ex. 20:9 KJV). This verse is a clear reminder about stewardship of time. Work is a good use of time, but laziness is a poor use of time. Proverbs 6:6 admonishes the lazy person to learn from the lowly ant. The ant works at the opportune time. That is the key . . . not how hard or how long you work, but how well you work at the right time.

In 2 Thessalonians 3:10 we read that those who will not work should not receive free food. Choosing the right occupation is a vital part of your time stewardship, but how you work and why you work is more important than where you work. In the New

Testament, slaves, who certainly did not choose their occupation, were admonished to work honestly, sincerely, and faithfully as though Jesus was their boss (Eph. 6:5-8). Working like that makes any job holy. It is doing the will of God as well as earning the pay of men and the reward of Christ.

We know how many hours are in a day and how many days are in a week, but we do not know how much time we have to manage. At any moment an accident or illness could take control of our time. Life is fragile, and we can be called to give account to our Lord at any moment. It is a relief to know that God, Who knows all, will guide us as we seek to be good stewards. A wise prayer is recorded in Psalm 90:12: "Teach us to number our days aright, that we may gain a heart of wisdom" (NIV).

Jesus is our perfect example of managing time. He always did the right thing at the right time. He did everything He was supposed to do in His life and ministry. From the cross He said, "It is finished," and in His prayer He said "I have finished the work which thou gavest me to do" (John 17:4*b* KJV). Jesus never let anyone but His Father set His agenda, though many tried. He said "I can of mine own self do nothing . . . because I seek not mine own will, but the will of the Father which hath sent me" (John 5:30 KJV).

When He faced Crucifixion He prayed to the Father, "Not my will but thine be done" (Luke 22:42*b* KJV). He was the most successful person who ever lived. Jesus had time for the multitudes and time for the individual. He stopped in the midst of a crowd to give blind Bartimaeus sight (Mark 10:46-52). Remember, Jesus lived in a time when there were no telephones, no fax machines, no air travel, no computers, and no wristwatches. Some may find a written schedule helpful; others are more comfortable with a different method of organizing their time. Whatever method you use, never let your schedule replace the dynamic will of God as His Spirit applies His Word to you!

**Reflections . . .**

1. Name as many of the Bible's definitions of time as you can think of.
2. Do you think every one has the same amount of time? Explain your answer.
3. Write a brief answer to each of the following questions:
   a. Why must a good steward redeem time?
   b. How can a good steward redeem time?
4. List characteristics of a good time manager based on biblical principles.

*T*herefore, since we are surrounded by such a great cloud of witnesses, let us throw off everything that hinders and the sin that so easily entangles, and let us run with perseverance the race marked out for us. Let us fix our eyes on Jesus, the author and perfecter of our faith, who for the joy set before him endured the cross, scorning its shame, and sat down at the right hand of the throne of God" (Heb. 12:1-2 NIV).

"Submit to one another out of reverence for Christ. Wives, submit to your husbands as to the Lord. Husbands, love your wives, just as Christ loved the church and gave himself up for her to make her holy. In this same way, husbands ought to love their wives as their own bodies. He who loves his wife loves himself. However, each one of you also must love his wife as he loves himself, and the wife must respect her husband. Children, obey your parents in the Lord, for this is right. 'Honor your father and mother'—which is the first commandment with a promise—'that it may go well with you and that you may enjoy long life on the earth.' Fathers, do not exasperate your children; instead, bring them up in the training and instruction of the Lord. Slaves, obey your earthly masters with respect and fear, and with sincerity of heart, just as you would obey Christ. Obey them not only to win their favor when their eye is on you, but like slaves of Christ, doing the will of God from your heart. Serve wholeheartedly, as if you were serving the Lord, not men, because you know that the Lord will reward everyone for whatever good he does, whether he is slave or free. And masters, treat your slaves in the same way. Do not threaten them, since you know that he who is both their Master and yours is in heaven, and there is no favoritism with him" (Eph. 5:21-22,25-26a,28,33; 6:1-9 NIV).

# 6

# Trusted with Relationships

Life and relationships are almost synonymous. We are part of a network of relationships that traces back to Adam, extends to all the people living today, and will continue throughout eternity. We are simultaneously blessed and cursed by our relationships. Responsibility goes with relationship. We are accountable to the people around us and to God. God revealed this to us very early in Genesis. After Cain intentionally killed his brother, Abel, the Lord said to Cain, " 'Where is your brother Abel?' 'I don't know,' he replied. 'Am I my brother's keeper?' The Lord said, 'What have you done? Listen! Your brother's blood cries out to me from the ground' " (Gen. 4:9-10 NIV). We are stewards of all our relationships including our heritage relationship with the past and the future, our family relationships, our civic relationships, and our church relationships.

**We are stewards of our heritage.** We are greatly influenced by all that has gone on before us. We owe a debt to all from whom we have inherited benefits. Many advantages afforded us as citizens of the United States came from the hard work and unselfish sacrifice of many people. Through a network of trade that we did not establish, the food we eat each day comes to our table from all over the world. The Bible is available in a language we can read because of people like John Wycliffe and others who were killed for their courageous translation efforts. Before them were the Hebrew people whom God chose to receive and record His revelation of Himself. Included in their number are those early Christians through whom God gave us the New Covenant. When Paul was preaching to the Gentiles, our ancestors were pagans who worshipped false gods and demons.

This debt calls for payment by our passing on to generations to come the faith once delivered to the saints. The Scriptures say it better than anyone else could: "Therefore, since we are surrounded by such a great cloud of witnesses, let us throw off everything that hinders and the sin that so easily entangles, and let us run with perseverance the race marked out for us. Let us fix our eyes on Jesus, the author and perfecter of our faith, who for the joy set before him endured the cross, scorning its shame, and sat down at the right hand of the throne of God" (Heb. 12:1-2 NIV). The words of a song inspire us: "May all who come behind us find us faithful!"

As strange as it may sound, we have a stewardship responsibility for dealing properly with all of the bad influence handed us. A pastor friend told me of a young couple he recently united in marriage. They had come to know Christ in a salvation experience. Before that, they were living together without marriage. In their serious efforts to follow Christ they decided they should be formally married. They also have shown integrity in other relationships. Their work and daily lifestyle reflect their loyalty to Christ. All of this is in contrast to their family backgrounds. His father was married to four different women and had several children by them. Her mother had several husbands, several children by them, and was in prison when this story unfolded. The young people were following their bad heritage until they met Christ. In His power they interrupted the cycle.

Some people find it necessary to seek Bible-based Christian counseling in their struggle to deal redemptively with the scars of their past. It is easy to blame those who wounded us, but blaming never solves the problem. We are not responsible for what they did to us; we are responsible for how we react. Our reaction shapes the quality of our life and what we pass on to those who come after us.

**We are stewards of family relationships.** The Bible has much to say about family relationships. Much of the book of Genesis is family stories. Sometimes family relationships were healthy; sometimes they were dysfunctional. Many passages contain commands and wise counsel for family matters. Two of the Ten Commandments deal directly with family issues, specifically parent-child and husband-wife relationships. "Honor your father and your mother, so that you may live long in the land the Lord your God is giving you" (Ex. 20:12 NIV). "You shall not commit adultery" (Ex. 20:14 NIV).

Husband-wife relationships are dealt with extensively. The excellent wife described in Proverbs 31:10-31 is worth more than jewels. She is trustworthy and does her husband good all her life. She is industrious in providing for her family. Interestingly enough, she is active in business affairs outside the home, but always for her family's benefit. She is a loving person who helps the poor. The way she dresses is an asset to her husband. She uses her mind to gain wisdom and discreetly passes it on. Her inner beauty is more important than her natural physical beauty. She has a strong and deep relationship with God and her family praises her.

A key passage on the marriage relationship is found in Ephesians 5:21-33. The beginning statement, which is often overlooked, is "Submit to one another out of reverence for Christ" (Eph. 5:21 NIV). As stewards of the marriage relationship each partner, both husband and wife, submits to meeting the other's needs. Each lives to make the other happy. The word translated "submission" in Ephesians 5:21 means "a voluntary attitude of giving in, cooperating, assuming responsibility, carrying a burden." Even friendships call for some "giving in." How much more the marriage relationship calls for cooperating or assuming responsibility. The marriage relationship is compared to Christ's love for the church, which took Him to His death on the cross. Submission, properly understood, is a key element in developing a successful marriage.

Parent-child relationships also get top priority. In the first book of the Bible, God compliments Abraham's effectiveness as a parent. "For I know him, that he will command his children and his household after him, and they shall keep the way of the Lord, to do justice and judgment; that the Lord may bring upon Abraham that which he hath spoken of him" (Gen.

18:19 KJV). The annual Passover Feast was a family affair; its message was to be explained to the children (Ex. 12:26). The Ten Commandments affirm that both the sins of wicked parents and the love and obedience of righteous parents affect children for generations to come (Ex. 20:5-6). Parents, especially fathers, are commanded to live by God's Word and teach it to their children so they may have a long and good life (Deut. 6:5-9; 11:18-21).

Parenting is a very serious issue. Malachi said the preaching of the prophet (John the Baptist) "will turn the hearts of the fathers to their children, and the hearts of the children to their fathers; or else I will come and strike the land with a curse" (Mal. 4:6 NIV). Our relationship with God is presented as a father-child relationship: "As a father has compassion on his children, so the Lord has compassion on those who fear him" (Psalm 103:13 NIV) and "the Lord disciplines those he loves, as a father the son he delights in" (Prov. 3:12 NIV). These are only a few typical examples.

The Bible takes the attitude that "children are an heritage of the Lord: and the fruit of the womb is his reward. As arrows are in the hand of a mighty man; so are children of the youth. Happy is the man that hath his quiver full of them: they shall not be ashamed, but they shall speak with the enemies in the gate" (Psalm 127:3-5 KJV). When God gives us children, He puts a priceless trust in our hands. Parents are stewards of that trust.

Parents find many examples in the Bible, good and bad, to help them in their stewardship. Both Jacob and Eli provide bad examples. Jacob's favoritism for Joseph caused many problems. Failing to properly discipline his sons caused the priest Eli great sorrow (1 Sam. 2:12-17,27-34).

Hannah and the Philippian jailor are positive examples. Hannah's unselfish love for her son Samuel was a strong influence in his rise to greatness (1 Sam. 1-3). The Philippian jailor's conversion to Christ was the key to the salvation of his entire family (Acts 16:31-34). One of the best examples is the faith of the grandmother and mother of Timothy. He caught their contagious faith and shone like a star in the New Testament (2 Tim. 1:5).

An excellent passage on the parent-child relationship is Ephesians 6:1-4. Children are reminded that they are to honor and obey their parents. God promises a long and good life to such children. Parents, especially fathers, are commanded not to provoke their children to the point of exasperation or discouragement, but to "bring them up in the training and instruction of the Lord" (Eph. 6:4b NIV). These are short statements that leave great latitude and demand much study and the seeking of wisdom from God.

The family (husband-wife and parent-child) relationship is the cornerstone of excellence in human civilization. This is a primary stewardship!

**Social relationships are important.** Christ said we are to be in the world but not of the world. Six of the Ten Commandments address our social relationships. We have stewardship responsibilities toward our friends, our neighbors, our community, the people we chance to meet, the people on the other side of town whom we have never met, and our government (city, county, state, federal). In all these relationships we are responsible for being salt and light. More than just relating, we are to be a positive force for good and for God.

Jesus affirmed that the second greatest commandment is "Thou shalt love . . . thy neighbor as thyself" (Luke 10:27 KJV). A man, hearing that, asked "Who is my neighbor?" Jesus replied with the story of the Good Samaritan. The answer to the question is this: your neighbor is the person in need, whether known or unknown, whether in your social class or not. Most people seem to know very little about the neighbors who live near them. If you believe God is in charge of your life, then you must acknowledge that your set of neighbors is no accident. They are your field for sowing seed, watering, cultivating, and harvesting.

If you were unsaved, how would you want your saved neighbor to treat you? The Golden Rule works very well here! Are your neighbors lonely, sad, depressed, grieving? Are some lost, addicted, or bound by some destructive sin? God has given you your neighbors; be salt and light. Giving money, even generously, will never substitute for your personal ministry.

We are stewards of our relationship to our government. Jesus said "Give to Caesar what is Caesar's" (Matt. 22:21 NIV). In our system of government we are responsible for every-

thing from voting to running for political office. We are to pay
our taxes, show respect for those in office, and obey the laws
(Rom. 13:1). We are to pray for our government leaders, especially that they will be saved (1 Tim. 2:1-8). God is on
record that He will give a positive answer to prayer for our
country (2 Chron. 7:14).

**Faithful stewardship of church relationships produces
good fruit.** Faithfulness calls for us to join a church soon after
we receive Christ as Savior, become a participating member of
the body we have joined, maintain a love relationship with our
fellow church members, and play a vital role on a team that is
assigned the task of making disciples of all nations.

If the words joining and member are problems for you, find
out what the Bible really says on this subject. You won't find
many direct commands, but you will find some assumptions
and examples. Jesus assumed that His followers would be a
part of a local body of believers when He gave the prescrip-
tion for handling fellowship problems in Matthew 18:15-17.
He said the third step in seeking reconciliation is "tell it to the
church." If you are not a member of a local church, how can
you obey that command?

Look at two examples of people becoming members. First,
baptized believers on the day of Pentecost were "added" to
the "church" (Acts 2:47). The word for church in that verse is
*ekklesia* and it means the "called out ones" or the "called together" ones. That word is translated throughout the New
Testament by the word church and is properly translated so in
the King James Version.

Second, when Paul attended the church at Jerusalem the
first time after his conversion the Bible says "he tried to join
the disciples" (Acts 9:26 NIV). The word translated join is
*kollaw*. It means to "glue together." That is what happens
when you join a church. You and they have a sense of belonging that does not come with simply "fellowshipping."

Add to the above the fact that the word member is used 14
times 1 Corinthians 12 to refer precisely to belonging to a local body of believers. The metaphor is that of a human body.
Its members are very firmly attached and committed to the
body. Joining a local body of believers (church) is the right
thing to do!

Joining is just the beginning of an active participating relationship. Every member has at least one spiritual gift for making the church body whole (1 Cor. 12:12-14). For a human body to function properly each member of the body must be attached, active, and working in harmony with the rest of the body (Eph. 4:16). The simple task of eating requires the cooperation of many parts of the body: the nervous system, the fingers, hands, wrists, arms, shoulder, eyes, mouth, teeth, tongue, and much more. So it is with a church.

Fellowship with other members must be maintained. It is normal for fellowship problems to arise. The scriptural record contains several reports of fellowship problems among the 12 apostles. Fellowship problems surfaced throughout the New Testament. Jesus gave us instructions for reconciling with one another (Matt. 5:23-24; 18:15-17).

For some strange reason we continue to be surprised by fellowship problems. Good stewardship calls for us to seek reconciliation promptly. That must be done by the offended parties. The pastor or the deacons are not effective substitutes in this matter. Some key statements are: "I was wrong"; "I am sorry"; "I ask you to forgive me"; "I forgive you." Those words must be said clearly and with feeling and integrity. Some people are afraid to forgive. Perhaps some do not understand that forgiveness means "I release the debt, I won't try to make you pay any more." Forgive is not saying "What you did was OK" nor "You are free to do it again." When we confess our sins to God He forgives, but He never says "What you did was OK" nor "You are free to do it again." He simply does not hold it against us any longer; He releases the debt. Forgiveness opens the door to reconciliation, but reconciliation and forgiveness are not the same. You can release the debt you have held against another even though that person is not willing to be reconciled.

Confronting a fellow believer is never easy. It can only be done effectively in the power of the Holy Spirit. Since He has commanded it, you can count on Him to help you do it. Your motive must be reconciliation. Getting even, manipulating, or playing power games must never be your intent. Actually, confronting a person with the intention of reconciliation is a compliment. It says "This relationship is important to me and I want to patch it up."

**Our most important relationship is with God.** That relationship is established when we repent of our sin and believe on the Lord Jesus Christ as Savior. Then God calls us "into fellowship with his Son" (1 Cor. 1:9). It is awesome to think that we can have fellowship with the same Jesus who fellowshipped with Peter, James, and John.

Our relationship to God is by spiritual birth, and it never changes. Our fellowship with God is constantly fluctuating. Fellowship rises and falls in direct proportion to our obedience. Sin breaks our fellowship. Anything that breaks our fellowship with Christ is a sin, whether it is considered as a sin or not. The Bible says, "If we claim to have fellowship with him yet walk in the darkness, we lie and do not live by the truth. But if we walk in the light, as he is in the light, we have fellowship with one another, and the blood of Jesus, his Son, purifies us from all sin" (1 John 1:6-7 NIV). Walking in the light, "as he is in the light," is the key to fellowship. When we break the fellowship, God wants to restore it and be reconciled. He made it very simple and spelled it out for us. "If we confess our sins, he is faithful and just and will forgive us our sins and purify us from all unrighteousness" (1 John 1:9 NIV).

Good stewardship of relationships includes establishing, cultivating, and maintaining relationships. We need good relationships. The people in our neighborhood need good relationships. Our families need good relationships. Our churches need good relationships. Our nation needs good relationships. We are the only ones who can meet these needs through the power of Christ.

# New Church Year
# New Adult Choir Music!

Now beginning rehearsals
On new music for:
- Homecoming: Oct. 23rd
- Joint Thanksgiving Service: Nov. 23rd
- Christmas Cantata: Dec. 18th

*Come join the fun and give of your heart to the Lord!*
Wednesday nights 8:00-9:00

**CHURCH-WIDE YARD SALE** on Sat., Oct. 8 in the FLC. If you have anything you would like to donate, please bring it to the FLC. Thank you

---

**You are invited to a Floating Baby Shower**
for Andrea & Brian Mutzabaugh
on Sunday, October 9, 2005 from 2:00-4:00 p.m.
in the Family Life Center
*They are having twin boys and are registered at Target*

---

**7:00 p.m. Sun., Oct. 9th Oakdale Baptist Church**
PCBC will meet at 7:00pm at Oakdale
Baptist Church for The **"Somebody's Praying Me Through"** Musical Program
(no 7:00pm service at PCBC)

---

**Sunday, October 23, 2005: Homecoming Day at PCBC**
●9:45-Sunday School  ●11:00-Morning Worship
●No 8:30am & 7:00pm services
Lunch in the Family Life Center after the morning service
**You are asked** to bring a covered dish, and a dessert, enough to share with others. The church is providing BBQ, hushpuppies & slaw. See Anne Lanier or call office to order fried chicken-$6.00
Invite friends & family!

**Reflections . . .**

1. Identify at least two negative and two positive impacts your personal heritage has made on you. Write a brief statement describing how you will be a good steward of all four.

2. Identify some ways you can develop better relationships
   a. in your marriage;
   b. in your parent-child relationships;
   c. with your friends;
   d. with your enemies;
   e. with your neighbors;
   f. with your church.

3. What definite things can you do to pass on a good heritage to those who come after you?

4. Write some ways you have been blessed by a word or deed from someone else; make plans to pass a similar blessing to someone else today.

*B*ut remember the Lord your God, for it is he who gives you the ability to produce wealth, and so confirms his covenant, which he swore to your forefathers, as it is today" (Deut. 8:18 NIV).

"Will a man rob God? Yet you rob me. But you ask, 'How do we rob you?' 'In tithes and offerings. Bring the whole tithe into the storehouse, that there may be food in my house. Test me in this,' says the Lord Almighty, 'and see if I will not throw open the floodgates of heaven and pour out so much blessing that you will not have room enough for it. Then all the nations will call you blessed, for yours will be a delightful land,' says the Lord Almighty" (Mal. 3:8,10,12 NIV).

"Give, and it will be given to you. A good measure, pressed down, shaken together and running over, will be poured into your lap. For with the measure you use, it will be measured to you" (Luke 6:38 NIV).

"Remember this: Whoever sows sparingly will also reap sparingly, and whoever sows generously will also reap generously. Each man should give what he has decided in his heart to give, not reluctantly or under compulsion, for God loves a cheerful giver. Now he who supplies seed to the sower and bread for food will also supply and increase your store of seed and will enlarge the harvest of your righteousness. You will be made rich in every way so that you can be generous on every occasion, and through us your generosity will result in thanksgiving to God" (2 Cor. 6-7,10-11 NIV).

# 7

# Trusted with Possessions

H onour the Lord with thy substance, and with the firstfruits of all thine increase: So shall thy barns be filled with plenty, and thy presses shall burst out with new wine" (Prov. 3:9-10 KJV). Reading these verses and the Scriptures on the previous page brings to the surface a flock of questions. What is "substance"? How much of our substance are we to use for God's honor? Why should we honor the Lord with our substance? How do we honor the Lord with our substance? What is the result of honoring the Lord with our substance? Let's answer these questions.

**What is substance?** Substance covers all our possessions, from the barest necessities to lavish wealth. The Hebrew word for substance means wealth, but wealth is such a relative term. We feel that wealth is more than we have at the time. The English definition for wealth includes all material objects that have economic utility, such as our house, automobile, clothing. The Hebrew word is used at times for all material possessions. Job considered anything gotten since his birth as wealth (Job 1:21). Every material thing we have is a trust from God and an excellent resource to do great things.

Notice that ownership is established by the adjective "thy" (Prov. 3:9 KJV). It is true that everything belongs to God, but

God has granted the right of possession to us in this life. Right of personal possession is recognized in the commandment "Thou shalt not steal" (Ex. 20:15 KJV). Our inner feelings about personal possession are formed during the first few years of life. Reality says that I cannot personally honor God with it unless it is personally belongs to me. So, substance is any personal possession that belongs to me.

**How much of our substance are we to use for God's honor?** All of it, of course . . . 100 percent. It seems easier to think of honoring God with a tithe, or 10 percent of what we have, and using the rest of it as we want to. To honor Him with some, and not with all, puts us into the Pharisee/hypocrite category. Though they tithed meticulously, they refused to honor God by helping their parents out of the rest of their wealth (Mark 7:10-13). All we have comes from His provision; we are accountable to Him for all of it. That's stewardship.

**Why should we honor God with our substance?** In the first place, God deserves to be honored simply because He has supplied all of our substance. When someone makes a significant gift to a college, that person is usually honored in some special way. A library may be named after the donor, or there may be a public recognition ceremony. Many colleges bear the name of the person who made their existence possible.

I heard of a man who had some rental houses. His widowed mother lived in one of them and paid him rent from her very limited income. When inflation raised the price of rentals, he demanded higher rent from his mother. She truly could not afford it and pleaded with him to have mercy. Surely he could have compassion on the mother who gave him birth and kept him alive with her tender care through his helpless years. Not him. He had her evicted! We react with horror to such action. Why, then, do we have difficulty with the thought that we should honor God with all our substance? We seem to find it so easy to forget where it comes from.

God reminded Israel of the danger of forgetfulness as they approached the promised land (Deut. 8:11-20). He identified four dangers of prosperity: a proud heart; forgetting God; taking credit for the prosperity; turning to other gods. God reminded them that He is the One who gives the power to make wealth.

The power to make wealth does not reside in us. This is made evident by the fact that many skilled, educated people work hard but live in poverty. Forgetting God's blessings leads directly to ruin. Israel fell into forgetfulness and experienced the ruin.

Secondly, other people need to see that Christians love God enough to honor Him with their substance. Our possessions provide us with that wonderful opportunity. Nothing reveals our true nature better than the way we use our possessions, including our money.

The idea of honoring God runs counter to the unsaved world's view of managing possessions. The world's system is based on getting; God's system is based on giving. God is a giver! He gave form to the earth when it was formless and void (Gen. 1:2). He gave life to every living creature. He gave Eve to Adam and Adam to Eve. He gave them dominion over the earth. "He himself gives all men life and breath and everything else" (Acts 17:25 NIV). He gave His only begotten Son so we would not perish but have everlasting life (John 3:16). Jesus gave His life on the cross for our sins. Salvation is a gift from God (Eph. 2:8-9). When Christians honor God by giving their possessions to Him and managing them according to God's plan, they reflect a likeness to God.

Which is the base of your economic plan, getting or giving? Getting easily turns to greed. In these times of credit cards, the getting mentality easily turns to excessive debt and oppressive payments. Everyone suffers when this happens: the one who "got" the things, the marriage, the family, and the people from whom the things were purchased. Problems compound, stress increases, depression sets in, and life loses its joy. Getting is basically selfish and is interested in pleasing self, not in honoring God.

Giving, on the other hand, develops us in likeness to God. It is in the system of giving that God meets all our needs. Parents give care, clothing, shelter, and security to their children. The children give honor to their parents. Parents give their children freedom to become the adults God wants them to be. The company gives the parents a job. The parents give the company their skills, time, and effort as if they were working for Christ. We give our life to Christ, and He gives us eternal life with Him. On and on the giving cycle goes, and more giving generates more blessing.

**How can we honor God with our substance?** We honor
God by making and using our substance in obedience to His
plan. His plan for our stewardship of possessions is clearly stated
in the Bible.

We honor God by making money and gaining possessions in
honorable ways. A Christian is out of place in an occupation that
contributes to addictions, moral perversion, loss of values, damage to family life, mental confusion, or otherwise damages people. Stealing, of any sort, is not honorable. Gambling is a form
of stealing; it greedily takes what belonged to another without
giving anything good in its place. Proverbs 13:11 tells us that
"dishonest money dwindles a way, but he who gathers money
little by little makes it grow" (NASB). The mandate to the
Christian is to work with our hands at "what is good" (Eph. 4:28
NASB). "Good" means the Christian's occupation should have a
positive effect on others. The Christian's motive in gaining possessions is that we may have something "to share with him who
has need" (Eph. 4:28 NIV).

We honor God by enjoying the substance God has supplied
to us (1 Tim. 6:17). Does it surprise you that God wants us to
enjoy what He has given us? Long ago, through the prophet
Jeremiah, God revealed that His plan for us includes prosperity, hope, and a bright future (Jer. 29:11 NIV). There are limits
and boundaries about how to enjoy our substance. It is never
to be done in a way that damages us or other people. It is
never to take the place of God. We ruin God's plan when we
transfer our trust from Him to our possessions or turn our joy
into selfish indulgence.

We honor God by using our substance to provide the necessities of life (1 Tim. 5:8). Failing to provide for our own is a de-
nial of the faith and makes us worse than unbelievers. Providing
for our own begins with the immediate family—father, mother,
son, daughter, brother, sister. It encompasses our extended family. Providing includes the material necessities of life, the mental
necessity of education, and the spiritual necessities. Jesus
scolded some scribes and Pharisees for failing to provide for
their needy parents by saying their possessions were dedicated
to God (Mark 7:9-13).

We honor God by paying our debts with our substance (Rom.
13:8). We must be very careful about making debts. In these
times of credit cards, it is very easy to get into more debt than

we can pay. We honor God by making the payments on time. Our witness is damaged if we are neglectful about paying our debts. The only unpaid debt we are allowed is the debt of love for one another.

We honor God by providing for the future with our substance (2 Cor. 12:14b). Proverbs 6:6-11 reminds us of the lowly ant who stores up food in the summer when it is available. That passage labels a person as lazy who refuses to use available substance to prepare for the lean times. In a dream, God told the Pharaoh of Egypt that he should use seven good harvest years to prepare for seven lean years (Gen. 41:1-39). Jesus did command us to avoid being preoccupied with seeking provision for tomorrow (Matt. 6:25-34). Our quest is to be His kingdom and righteousness. He promised if we would seek first the kingdom (rule) of God, He would meet all of tomorrow's needs. It is possible that God's care for tomorrow could come in the form of a surplus today, as it did for Egypt. Jesus did warn us against treasuring material things in our hearts (Matt. 6:19-24). This addresses our attitude toward savings and insurance, not the mechanics of saving and buying insurance.

One October, while in Colorado hunting elk with my son, we saw a flock of sparrows eating the seeds left over from summer. God's way of taking care of them was by growing a surplus amount of seeds during the summer. Good steward-ship calls for properly managing the surplus. Jesus told the apostles to pick up the remains after feeding the 5,000 "that nothing be lost" (John 6:12 KJV). Both worry and wastefulness are poor stewardship. If God provides more than you need to-day, He either wants you to give it away or use it to provide for tomorrow. He can lead you to manage it well if you are putting Him first.

Providing for the future also includes laying up treasure in heaven (Matt. 6:19-21). First we must believe on the Lord Jesus Christ as our personal Savior. Then we must use the substance He provides for us to do eternal things.

We honor God when we give of our substance. Though this is really the first way we honor God with our substance, I men-tioned it last so you will be aware that there are many ways to honor God with your possessions. Proverbs 3:9 calls for the "firstfruits," or giving to God first before we do anything else with our possessions.

Her first name was May. Her husband left her with two small girls to raise. The only job May could get was working in a laundry. The pay was very small, hardly enough to meet their needs. One night she hosted a prayer meeting for the coming revival. When she opened her Bible to give the devotional, her Sunday School offering envelope fell out. She blushed a bit and explained that she always put her tithe in her Bible first so she wouldn't spend it for other things. God was first in her heart! God did meet May's needs and helped her raise two fine girls to adulthood.

Clearly the tithe (10 percent) belongs to the Lord (Lev. 27:30). No where in the Bible does He revoke the tithe. Malachi 3:9 informs us that using the tithe for ourselves will bring a curse. Are you aware that many Christians are living "under a curse" financially? If you want to know what it is like to live under that curse, read Haggai 1:5-10. People who are living under a curse often run out of money before needs are met and expect more than they receive. On the other hand, God promised a blessing to those who would bring the tithe into the storehouse (Mal. 3:8-12). The blessing extends to the nation. How many of our national economic problems are caused by people not tithing and not being good stewards of the rest of their possessions?

Christians, living under the new covenant, cannot stop with the tithe. The Christian's economic system is described in 2 Corinthians 9:6-15, as having six elements: (1) sow (give) bountifully and you will reap bountifully; (2) purpose in your heart to be a cheerful, generous giver like God (vv. 7,15); (3) God will enable you to give generously (vv. 8,10,11); (4) God will increase the harvest of your righteousness (vv. 6,11$b$); (5) the needs of others will be supplied (v. 12); (6) people will glorify God because of your giving.

**What are results of honoring God with our substance?**
Proverbs 3:10 says, "So shall thy barns be filled with plenty, and thy presses shall burst out with new wine" (KJV). Your needs, and those of your family, will be met. Your work will take on new meaning. Managing your possessions will become productive. Your church will have enough money to finance everything God leads them to do. Your witness to the unsaved will be more effective. You will enjoy a real fellowship with Christ in your daily life. All your possessions will take on a sacred meaning. At the end you will hear the Lord say "Well done."

**Reflections . . .**

1. Make an inventory of the "substance" God has trusted to you.
2. Clarify in your own mind and heart two reasons you should honor God with the "substance" He has trusted to you.
3. This chapter stated six ways to honor God with your substance.
   a. How many of them can you name without looking?
   b. Can you think of other specific ways you can honor God with your substance?

*You also, like living stones, are being built into a spiritual house to be a holy priesthood, offering spiritual sacrifices acceptable to God through Jesus Christ. For in Scripture it says: 'See, I lay a stone in Zion, a chosen and precious cornerstone, and the one who trusts in him will never be put to shame.' Now to you who believe, this stone is precious. But to those who do not believe, 'The stone the builders rejected has become the capstone,' and, 'A stone that causes men to stumble and a rock that makes them fall.' They stumble because they disobey the message—which is also what they were destined for. But you are a chosen people, a royal priesthood, a holy nation, a people belonging to God, that you may declare the praises of him who called you out of darkness into his wonderful light. Once you were not a people, but now you are the people of God; once you had not received mercy, but now you have received mercy"* (1 Peter 2:5-10 NIV).

# 8

# Trusted with Position

Do you have a responsible position? Before answering too hastily, remember that responsible positions include those of parent, child, sibling, employee and employer, child of God, ambassador of Christ, even being sheep among wolves. Your primary responsibility is to God! You are also responsible to people who are affected by how you manage your position. One of the great "position" passages is found in 1 Peter 2:5-10. Several positions are mentioned; a living stone in a spiritual house; a holy priesthood; a chosen race; a royal priesthood; a people for God's own possession; the people of God. Because priesthood is basic to good stewardship in all other positions, we need to take two necessary steps; first, acknowledge our position; then, accept our position.

**Acknowledge your priesthood.** I believe everyone has a responsible position, but few realize it. The Bible declares that every saved person is a priest (1 Peter 2:5-10). The same God who set aside Aaron's descendants as holy priests in the Old Testament has declared you are a priest. You are both a holy (v. 5) and royal (v. 9) priest. The same God who instructed Samuel to anoint David as royal King of Israel has made you royalty. Your priesthood is superior to the Old Testament priesthood. They were holy priests; you are both holy and royal.

Christ qualified you to be a priest through several spiritual actions (1 Peter 1:1-10). He chose you; He sanctified you through the work of the Spirit and the sprinkling of His blood; He caused you to be born again; He saved you. You will find some of these elements in His choosing of the Old Testament priest.

You may say, "I don't feel like a priest." Let me ask you, "How does a priest feel?" You have been a priest since you were saved. Have you ever acknowledged it?

**Accept your priesthood.** One may acknowledge the reality of being a priest yet reject the role. Accepting means you are willing to serve as a priest. But what does a saved, New Testament priest do?

In the past, the emphasis was almost exclusively on our right to approach God for ourselves, without any other human mediator. Though this is a valid application of our priesthood, it is only one part of the issue.

Our focal passage in 1 Peter 2 assigns to us two positive actions that are great and wonderful. As a priest, we offer up "spiritual sacrifices acceptable to God by Jesus Christ" (1 Peter 2:5 NIV). We also "proclaim the excellencies of Him who has called you out of darkness into His marvelous light" (1 Peter 2:9 NASB). It will ignite your sense of purpose to examine each of these carefully.

We are to offer up spiritual sacrifices, acceptable to God. We can offer the sacrifice of service in a way that God will accept and bless. We can offer our gifts of tithes and offerings, which God will accept and bless. We can give a thirsty person a cup of cold water, and God will bless it. We can offer the "sacrifice of praise" (Heb. 13:15 NIV) as we join in congregational singing at church, and God will accept it and bless us. You can present your body to God as a living sacrifice and discover the will of God in fulfillment. Understanding this will enliven your participation in the worship services at your church. When you sing, pray, give, testify, teach, and support you are offering a sacrifice to God just as real as those bulls and goats offered by the Old Testament priest.

God does not accept every sacrifice. He rejected Cain's sacrifice. He rejected the sacrifices of the people in the days of Isaiah (Isa. 1:10-15; 66:1-4). In Proverbs we read "The sacrifice of the wicked is an abomination to the Lord: but the prayer of the upright is his delight" (Prov. 15:8 NRSVB). God rejected the sacrifices of the Israelites in Amos' time (Amos 5:21-23). But you, a holy and royal priest, can offer Him acceptable sacrifices. Your co-workers, family, neighbors, friends, and acquaintances may be like the people of Judah, Jerusalem, and Israel. Their prayers and offerings may be repulsive to God because they have not received Him and are living in rebellion against Him. Because God accepts your prayers, they need you to pray for them. Do you know some people who need the ministry of a God-appointed, holy, and royal priest? Awaken to your position and God-appointed role! Be a good steward of that responsibility.

You are also to "proclaim the excellencies of Him who has called you out of darkness into His marvelous light" (1 Peter 2:9 NASB). He called you out of the darkness of lostness and sin, into the marvelous light of His salvation, to be an example of His excellent work. The world does not consider Christ to be excellent. They blame Him for all the bad things that happen. They criticize Him for not making things better, not stopping wars, not ending child abuse, and allowing crime. They question the truthfulness of His Word. They have little use for the gospel of His death and Resurrection. They think being saved is strange and impractical. Christ needs for you to show them He is truly excellent by living a converted life. They need to know that salvation works in the daily lives of ordinary people. They need to see that Christ's salvation solves addiction problems, changes criminals to loving, productive citizens, makes honest people out of liars and shoplifters, cleanses adulterers from guilt and sinful activity, makes people better parents, turns greedy people into giving people. They need to know that personal conversion is God's solution to war, crime, and abuse. You are in a better position than even a "professional priest" to show the world that salvation does more than make people go to church.

Wouldn't you agree that such a priestly ministry is needed? Jesus, our great High Priest, practiced this kind of ministry. He went about doing good. He touched people where they hurt. He ministered to their "felt needs," and they opened the door to His eternal ministry. Jesus commanded us to be salt and light!

**Practice your priesthood.** Your employment position is an excellent place to begin. Whether you are the top executive or the least-paid employee, your priestly ministry is needed and effective. Your body is a temple of the Holy Spirit (1 Cor. 6:19-20). Wherever you are, there is a holy temple indwelt by God. I am not suggesting you begin to conduct "worship services" while the boss expects you to be working. You show how excellent Christ is by your attitude toward the others who work around you.

Does the love of Christ radiate from you? Does the fruit of the Spirit grow on the tree of your life? People are impressed with love, joy, peace, patience, kindness, goodness, faithfulness, gentleness, and self-control. When they notice, simply mention that Christ has corrected your attitude. By proving that saved people make excellent employees, you show the excellence of Christ. The Bible says we are to work as if Christ was our employer (Eph. 6:5-7). Those are the sacrifices that shine the light of Christ into the darkness where you work.

Your family, the primary place to practice your priesthood, is also the most difficult place because your family knows the "real" you. No Christian is perfect. It is acceptable to be imperfect, admit you are imperfect, and continue to grow. It is not acceptable to claim perfection when everyone else knows better. Your family needs your priestly ministry of prayer, kindness, love, and listening. If they are not saved, Christ will shine through.

Saved family members need the ministry of other saved family members. Husbands and wives show Christ's excellence by loving and honoring one another (1 Peter 3:1-7). Parents show the excellence of Christ by bringing up children in the discipline and nurture of the Lord. Children minister as priests by honoring their parents. Even "sibling rivalry" can be overcome by the application of God's grace and acceptance. Problem-solving skills that reflect what Christ taught about confrontation, confession, and forgiveness are excellent priestly activities. Whatever your position in the family, you have a priestly role to fulfill that will minister the grace of God.

Your position in public life and citizenship calls for the practice of your priesthood. Every Christian is a citizen; some are also elected or employed officials. Integrity, honesty, and fairness are desperately needed. We need public officials who are Christian in their conduct. What a great opportunity to let Jesus shine! In our government, the officials reflect the people who elect them. Our nation needs a turning to God and His values. Christians, leading the way, can show that Christ's salvation makes excellent citizens. When we vote, when we pay our taxes, as we drive down the road, when we are dealing with public officials, we can prove Christ is excellent by letting Him control our conduct and conversation.

When you are suffering, your position is one of the best platforms for exerting your priestly influence. A sufferer is expected to be mean tempered, dirty tongued, and generally out of sorts. I visited the hospital room of one of our church members. She was not a "happy camper." She was fussing about the nurses, the care, the food, the temperature, and everything else. When the nurse responded to her ring, I stood and listened as she attacked that nurse without mercy. Then she paused and said, "By the way, I want you to meet my pastor," and introduced me. I did not want that nurse to know that the patient was a member of my church or any church for that matter! Her witness was completely counterproductive.

When a person who is in pain displays the spirit of Christ, patience, compassion for others, and faith in God, the excellence of Christ's salvation shines brightly. Christ, Who died on the cross and prayed for those who nailed Him there, can give you the grace to have a sweet and gentle spirit in the midst of suffering. Such a ministry turns a hospital room into a cathedral, and a bed of suffering into an eloquent pulpit. The Apostle Paul learned to glory in infirmities (2 Cor. 12:7-10). Think about how many people have been ministered to by Job though he has been dead for thousands of years!

Your position with your associates, whether they be your Sunday School class, your Women on Mission group, your neighbors, or any other group, gives you a ministry responsibility. Your place in the group may be leader, follower, or quiet supporter. Each role is vital to the group; each position offers an opportunity to show that Christ is excellent. Letting Him control your otherwise uncontrollable tongue will exert great and positive influence. We must never be content with merely avoiding evil. We must exert a positive message of how excellent Christ is. Here is some great advice: "Do not let any unwholesome talk come out of your mouths, but only what is helpful for building others up according to their needs, that it may benefit those who listen" (Eph. 4:29 NIV).

Even the position you have with your enemies provides a need for responsible, Christ-directed action. Your enemies may be those in faraway places, but they are more likely to be in your own household (Matt. 10:36). Jesus commanded us: "Love your enemies, bless them that curse you, do good to them that hate you, and pray for them which despitefully use you, and persecute you" (Matt. 5:44 KJV). Your enemies oppose you with hostility. To curse someone is to call for evil to befall that person. Hate is to maintain an attitude of hatred. Despitefully use means to insult, falsely accuse, threaten, treat abusively, or insult. Persecute means to make one flee. To this vile treatment Jesus said, love them with the love described in John 3:16, invoke the blessings of God on them, and pray for them because then you act like your heavenly Father. Jesus practiced this toward His enemies; He can enable you to do it also. At times I pray, "Lord, I cannot love and bless and pray for this person in my strength; give me your love for them." When I pray like that I remember that Jesus suffered on that cross for my enemies just as surely as He suffered for me. He loves them and with His help, I can love them.

Your church position calls for your priestly ministry. Fulfill the responsibility that Christ and your fellow Christians have placed on you. Do it with a spirit of gentleness, not manipulation or haughtiness. Follow, with a gentle spirit, the leadership of those who occupy the positions. Pray for one another. Let Christ purge out all selfish motives and competitiveness. "Make every effort to maintain the unity of the Spirit through the bond of peace" (Eph. 4:3 NIV). Go to church to render a ministry, and you will be ministered to abundantly (Heb. 10:24-25). Encourage others and you will find encouragement!

Is Christ excellent to you? Then show it to others! Be a good steward of your responsibilities.

**Reflections . . .**

1. Read again 1 Peter 2:5-10, then write your own paraphrase of these verses.
2. Take time right now to prayerfully accept your priesthood from God, even though your understanding of it may be inadequate.
3. Ask God to help you learn how He wants you to practice your priesthood.
4. Write a list of ways you personally can practice the responsibilities of your priesthood.

*I do not want you to be unaware, brothers, that I planned many times to come to you (but have been prevented from doing so until now) in order that I might have a harvest among you, just as I have had among the other Gentiles. I am obligated both to Greeks and non-Greeks, both to the wise and the foolish. That is why I am so eager to preach the gospel also to you who are at Rome. I am not ashamed of the gospel, because it is the power of God for the salvation of everyone who believes: first for the Jew, then for the Gentile. For in the gospel a righteousness from God is revealed, a righteousness that is by faith from first to last, just as it is written: 'The righteous will live by faith' " (Rom. 1:13-17 NIV).*

*"Therefore, if anyone is in Christ, he is a new creation; the old has gone, the new has come! All this is from God, who reconciled us to himself through Christ and gave us the ministry of reconciliation: that God was reconciling the world to himself in Christ, not counting men's sins against them. And he has committed to us the message of reconciliation" (2 Cor. 5:17-19 NIV).*

*"Then Jesus came to them and said, 'All authority in heaven and on earth has been given to me. Therefore go and make disciples of all nations, baptizing them in the name of the Father and of the Son and of the Holy Spirit, and teaching them to obey everything I have commanded you. And surely I am with you always, to the very end of the age" (Matt. 28:18-20 NIV).*

# 9

# Trusted With the Gospel

The crown jewels of Great Britain comprise one of the world's greatest collections of wealth. A few years ago my wife and I went to the Tower of London to see that awesome display. I never imagined precious gems like the ones we saw that day even existed. Huge diamonds seemed almost alive as they radiated the colors of the rainbow. Rubies and emeralds, by the score, added their brilliance. Pearls—rare, large, unique, and abundant—glowed as if lighted from within.

Security was intense. Men, armed and alert, were stationed every few feet. The potential of theft was always on their minds. Electronic surveillance aided them in their duty of keeping that treasure safe. The line of viewers was kept moving. Taking pictures was forbidden, and we were regularly reminded of this.

The sight of so much beautiful wealth moved me deeply. I thought of the "riches of God's grace" (Eph. 1:7 NASB). Of course, the riches of God's grace are not material things like jewels and gold. In heaven, we are told, the streets are paved with gold, and the foundations garnished with precious gems. God has riches much more valuable than jewels and money!

What do you think is God's most precious possession? What is dearest to His heart? To what has God given His energy and the thoughts of His unsearchable mind across the eons of time?

What treasure do the angels in heaven guard with intense security? What causes rejoicing to break out in the presence of the angels? What is His greatest concern?

The answer is found in a single verse of Scripture—John 3:16. The salvation of the lost is dearest to God's heart. Before He laid the foundation of the earth His unsearchable intelligence devised the plan for the lost to be saved (Matt. 25:34; Eph. 1:4; Heb. 4:3; 1 Peter 1:20; Rev. 13:8; 17:8). Very dear to God's heart is His only Son. Yet He said no to the plea of His Son from Gethsemane: "My Father, if it is possible, let this cup pass from me" (Matt. 26:39 KJV). The Scripture says "with God all things are possible" (Matt. 19:26 NIV). Yes, it was possible to let the cup pass from His Son. But it was not possible to save the lost and spare His Son the death of the cross. God chose to save the lost! The rest of Jesus' prayer was "Yet not as I will, but as you will" (Matt. 26:39 NIV). God's eternal will is to save the lost. The angels "long to look into these things" (1 Peter 1:12*b* NIV). They announced the birth of the Savior. They ministered to Him during His temptation. More than twelve legions of angels were ready to protect Him from the Crucifixion. The voice of the archangel will announce the return of Christ. "There is rejoicing in the presence of the angels of God over one sinner who repents" (Luke 15:10 NIV). God's greatest concern is expressed in His message through Ezekiel: "Say to them, 'As surely as I live, declares the Sovereign Lord, I take no pleasure in the death of the wicked, but rather that they turn from their ways and live' " (Ezek. 33:11 NIV).

The gospel of salvation is a vital part of God's greatest treasure. God has trusted us with that gospel. Jesus in His life, death, and Resurrection provided the gospel. When He returned to His Father, He put it into our hands. If we are not good stewards, then His lifetime of work, His sacrifice on the cross, and His powerful Resurrection will be for naught.

If we are poor stewards of our body, we will suffer physically. If we fail in stewardship of our mind, we will suffer mentally. If we waste our talents and time, we will miss valuable opportunities. Mishandling relationships will cause us social suffering. Poor stewardship of our possessions will cause us financial problems. But if we are not good stewards of the gospel, people will miss heaven and suffer in hell forever! If we are not good stewards the lost cannot be saved (Acts 4:12)! These statements compare the very important with the most important. The stewardship of the gospel is our most important area of stewardship!

**What is the gospel?** As you know, the word gospel, meaning "good news," is a very important word in the Scriptures. The Bible tells us that Jesus went to Galilee preaching "the good news of God" (Mark 1:14 NIV). Peter and John preached the "gospel in many Samaritan villages" (Acts 8:25 NIV). Paul wrote, "woe is unto me, if I preach not the gospel!" (1 Cor. 9:16*b* KJV). What is this good news that they were preaching? The essence of God's good news is in three statements recorded in 1 Corinthians 15:3-4: "Christ died for our sins . . . he was buried, and he was raised on the third day" (NIV).

Christ died for our sins. Though "the wages of sin is death" (Rom. 6:23), the good news is that Christ died in our place and paid the death penalty for our sins. God made that sacrifice, and it is complete payment for all our sins. Because of Jesus' death we have solid hope that God will forgive our sins when we confess them. Therefore, God has "justified" us (Rom. 3:23-26). Being justified includes being declared not guilty!

Jesus really died. The Roman soldier, trained in the art of killing, stood before the helpless body of Jesus. He had all the time he wanted to aim carefully and thrust his sharp spear into Jesus' side, slicing and tearing His vital organs. The Roman officer in charge, being very familiar with death, certified to Pilate that Jesus was indeed dead. "Since the children have flesh and blood, He too shared in their humanity so that by His death He might destroy him who holds the power of death—that is, the devil—and free those who all their lives were held in slavery by their fear of death" (Heb. 2:14-15 NIV).

When Christ was buried, they sealed His body in a rock tomb. He was not in an intensive care unit where He was hooked up to life support systems. Someday, unless Christ returns first, they will lay our body in a casket, carry it out to a cemetery, and bury it six feet in the ground. If you want to shop for the abode where your body will spend the most time, shop at the mortuary!

Jesus won the victory over our greatest enemy, death. Good news! We can face death and burial without fear. Christ has proven that burial of the body is not to be dreaded for those who commit their spirit into the hands of God! Hallelujah!

Christ was raised from the dead! Have you let that good news sink deep into your heart? No news can be as good as that news! During His ministry, Jesus restored several people to this life—the son of the widow of Nain, Jairus' twelve-year-old daughter, Lazarus, and others. But they came back to life on this side of glory. Jesus was raised on the other side of death, never to die again. He said, "Because I live, you also will live" (John 14:19*b* NIV). His Resurrection is God's promise that we shall be raised from the dead when Christ returns (1 Thess. 4:13-18). We will have a new and perfect body, a body like His (1 John 3:2). We will never die or suffer any kind of pain again. Forever we will worship and serve our Lord! Good news! Hope!

**The gospel is for everyone.** The gospel is for children who grow up in a Christian home. Last Sunday, a youth of fourteen responded to the invitation to publicly confess His faith in Christ. He grew up in a Christian home and in our church. His mother's father was a pastor. Indeed, the gospel is for our children raised in our Christian homes.

The gospel is for people who grow up in America. A few months ago, a young couple in their early 20s came to my office to discuss wedding plans. I discovered the man had not been saved, nor was he raised in a Christian home. He did say that his sister died about a year ago, and he had been thinking a lot about God since them. When I asked if he would like for me to take the Bible and show him how to be saved, he said yes. I read Romans 3:23, 6:23, and 10:9. I told him that when he believed in his heart that Christ died for his sin and arose from the dead to be his Savior—believed this enough to make Jesus his Lord—he would be saved. Immediately he said "I make Him my Lord." I did not even get to the part about calling on the name of the Lord! He was ready for the gospel that is for people raised in America.

The gospel is for people who have committed unspeakable crimes and wickedness. I was sitting in a visitor's cell at the county jail, talking with a teenager who had participated in a gang murder of three drunk men. I took him down the "Roman road." Then we knelt and through his tears he confessed his sin to Christ, asking Him to forgive and save him. When we finished praying, while we were still on our knees, I had him read again these words: "For whosoever shall call upon the name of the

Lord shall be saved" (Rom. 10:13 KJV).

I asked, "Did you call on His name?"

He replied "Yes."

I asked, "Did He save you?"

He replied "Yes, yes!" At that very moment the jailor opened the door and brought in his mother and dad. He jumped from his knees, hugged them, and shouted, "Jesus has just saved me!" The gospel is for sinners!

The gospel is for people of every race and culture. While in an evangelistic crusade in Sapporo, Japan, I noticed a beautiful Japanese young lady who responded to the invitation. In the counseling room my interpreter told me her story. She said, "I am a stewardess for All Japan Airlines. We fly into Sapporo one day each month and spend the night here before we return to our point of origin. I saw the advertisement of the crusade at the hotel and decided to attend. Tonight you preached on a woman who had a thirst in her soul that was filled with Christ (John 4). I have had that thirst for a long time. I have gone to the temples and left thirsty. I fly with the wealthy people and realize they have the same thirst, so it cannot be filled with riches. Tonight, when I asked Jesus to come into my soul and be my Savior, the thirst was satisfied." The gospel is for everyone!

"For God so loved the world . . . that whosoever believeth in him should not perish, but have everlasting life" (John 3:16 KJV). "Christ Jesus came into the world to save sinners" (1 Tim. 1:15 NIV). "All have sinned" (Rom. 3:23a NIV). Jesus commanded us to "Go into all the world and preach the good news to all creation" (Mark 16:15 NIV). We do not know who will receive and who will reject. We do know that everyone must hear the gospel. Our stewardship is not complete until every one has heard. Our personal stewardship is not complete until we have done all that is possible, in the power of God's Spirit, to tell everyone. Billy Graham recently sought to preach the gospel to everyone on earth. He, one man, succeeded more than any other man. Yes, it took an army of technicians and organizers, but he set it in motion and saw it through, at age 76! Our efforts must include telling, praying, and sending.

**We are stewards of the gospel.** Christ gave us the gospel and left it up to us to declare it to everyone. What an awesome stewardship! It is awesome in its potential for great glory or great shame. Great glory is a multitude that no man can count, from every race and nation, standing in heaven and praising God for saving them (Rev. 7:9-10). Great shame is ours if we do not proclaim the gospel to every person on earth. If we do not tell them, they will not be saved. The Bible asks "how can they believe in the one of whom they have not heard?" (Rom. 10:14 NIV). Two passages in Ezekiel suggest horrible guilt if we are unfaithful (Ezek. 3:17-21; 33:7-9).

A mockingbird has built a nest in a vine in our backyard. Because the vine is only about five feet above ground level, I can walk by and see into the nest. She has been sitting on four eggs. Today they hatched. I happened to walk by the nest while the mother was gone to find food. The tiny birds are so new they have very little shape, but one bird had its mouth open to the sky, asking for food. Today the bird cannot make a sound. One day it will sing beautiful songs and soar through the air with ease, but now it is just groping for something to eat. From a distance I watched the mother return to the nest, carrying a bit of food in her beak. Those birds will never fly or sing if she does not feed them. They will die.

The unsaved are like those tiny birds. They have a hunger but do not know it is for Christ. They have no idea how life will soar when He sets them free. They do not know the songs of glory that can fill their hearts and minds. They have no hope of heaven. They simply stand with the mouths of their souls open, waiting for some responsible gospel steward to give them the bread of life. If we fail to be good stewards of the gospel, they will never be free; they will never sing; they will perish in their sin.

If, however, we are faithful in proclaiming the gospel we will bear much good fruit. Souls will be saved forever, and we will rejoice with them in glory. Churches will be built up. Christ will be glorified. Heaven will rejoice. Family life will be improved. Children will have better parents, and parents will have better children. Our nation will be blessed. Our hearts will sing, and we will hear our Lord say, "Well done, thou good and faithful steward."

**Reflections . . .**

1. What is the gospel?
2. Plan specific steps you will take in becoming a better steward of the gospel.
3. Review the nine things God has trusted us with (see chapter titles). Rewrite this list using your own words; add additional areas if you think of them. Arrange your list in your own priority order.

*I am the vine; you are the branches. If a man remains in me and I in him, he will bear much fruit; apart from me you can do nothing" (John 15:5 NIV).*

"When Peter saw this, he said to them: 'Men of Israel, why does this surprise you? Why do you stare at us as if by our own power or godliness we had made this man walk?' " (Acts 3:12 NIV)

"For God did not give us a spirit of timidity, but a spirit of power, of love and of self-discipline" (2 Tim. 1:7 NIV).

"If anyone serves, he should do it with the strength God provides, so that in all things God may be praised through Jesus Christ" (1 Peter 4:11b NIV).

"But we have this treasure in jars of clay to show that this all-surpassing power is from God and not from us" (2 Cor. 4:7 NIV).

"The acts of the sinful nature are obvious: sexual immorality, impurity and debauchery; idolatry and witchcraft; hatred, discord, jealousy, fits of rage, selfish ambition, dissensions, factions and envy; drunkenness, orgies, and the like. I warn you, as I did before, that those who live like this will not inherit the kingdom of God. But the fruit of the Spirit is love, joy, peace, patience, kindness, goodness, faithfulness, gentleness and self-control. Against such things there is no law" (Gal. 5:19-23 NIV).

# 10

# Trusted with the Secret of Successful Stewardship

Can you imagine a woman who has never seen a vacuum cleaner? This woman, who has no idea how a vacuum cleaner works, has been told that she needs a vacuum to clean her new carpet properly. So she locates a store, buys a vacuum, and takes it home. Though she runs it back and forth over the carpet, the lint and debris from the installation remain on the carpet. She tries running it back and forth faster and faster, but the carpet is still not cleaned. Next she tries pushing it forward only, but that is no better. Then she drags it backward, but still she sees no improvement.

She decides that it must take a long time of pushing it back and forth, so she spends hours doing this, without success. She is so frustrated that she even considers running it upside down, but that is beyond logic. Finally she calls the store to report that the vacuum does not work. The salesman responds by coming to her house. The first thing he does is remove the power cord from the handle and plug it into the socket. The woman says, "I wondered what that cord was on there for." He turns on the switch and the motor hums. The woman asks, "What is that noise?" Then he begins to vacuum the floor, with obvious success.

That story is so absurd it borders on insulting our intelligence. Yet many Christians are trying to be good stewards in the same way that woman was trying to vacuum the floor, without the proper power. We make every effort possible in our own strength to do it right, but we experience consistent failure. In the area of body stewardship we often slip into laziness—eating too much, failing to exercise, or taking part in some activity that violates stewardship. Our mind is so easily distracted from right thinking. We try to be good stewards of our time, but seldom seem to do the right thing at the right time.

There is a real struggle between being a good steward of our possessions and being possessed by them. In witnessing, we become fearful and often fail altogether. Add to all of this the problem we have with motive. Stewardship cannot be right if it comes from mechanical, legalistic, or selfish motives. Where can we find the power to fulfill our trust? We need to learn to switch from our own power to God's power.

It took Jesus about three years to get the apostles to understand they could not serve God in their own strength. He used many methods. When He sent them out to evangelize, He gave them "authority to do it" (Matt. 10:1). He let them experience failure in their efforts to heal the demoniac son. Jesus came on the scene, rebuked the demon, and the boy was cured instantly (Matt. 17:14-20).

When He asked them how they would feed 5,000 hungry men, with their limited lunch of only five loaves and two fish, they admitted their inability. So, in their presence, Jesus blessed the bread and fish and fed the 5,000. Again He gave them an experience of switching from their own power to God's power, but they failed to see it.

The night before His Crucifixion, Jesus said, "I am the vine; you are the branches. If a man remains in me and I in him, he will bear much fruit; apart from me you can do nothing" (John 15:5 NIV). Note His statement: "apart from me you can do nothing." The word is *nothing*, not some things or very little but *nothing!* In Gethsemane, Jesus commanded His disciples to "Watch and pray, that ye enter not into temptation: the spirit indeed is willing, but the flesh is weak" (Matt. 26:41 KJV). Notice what Jesus said about the flesh: it is weak. Peter rejected the idea and did his best on his own to defend Jesus with his sword, but Jesus rebuked Peter's actions. A few hours later, Peter denied he even knew Christ. He went out greatly disappointed in himself, with a broken heart, in utter defeat.

After His Resurrection, Jesus commissioned Peter to feed His sheep and commanded all of them to make disciples of all nations. Then He sternly warned them to wait until they were empowered by the Holy Spirit (Luke 24:49; Acts 1:8). Though He had taught them and trained them, they were not to try to serve Him in their own power. He would supply the power; they would supply submission, willingness, and obedience. When they finally stopped trying to serve Christ in their own strength, and submitted to God's power, they became successful, powerful, fruitful stewards.

This is obviously a difficult lesson for all of us to learn. Paul lamented the weakness of the flesh in his letter to the Romans (Rom. 7:18b-19, 24-25a NIV). Only Christ can give us the power to do right, to witness, or to be a good steward! In our own power we do the "works of the flesh" (Gal. 5:19-21). Only in God's power is the fruit of the Spirit produced (Gal. 5:22-23).

**All power comes from God.** Since the beginning God has possessed all power and the authority to exercise it. He exercised His power in creating the heavens and the earth (Gen. 1:1). Since the creation He has demonstrated His power by maintaining and governing His creation. He manifested His awesome power when He raised Jesus from the dead. At the end of the age, God will manifest His power by destroying evil and by establishing complete righteousness and justice.

God has endowed His creations with limited power. For example, gravity gives power to falling rocks; atoms possess atomic power. Chemical and physical power are obvious. Some of God's creations are endowed with life and the power of procreation. Animals have muscle power. Man has amazing power: mental, physical, social, procreative. God also assigns nations the power to govern. God's gifts of power are evident all around us.

**Christ has all power.** Christ displayed God's power during His lifetime, healing the sick, making the blind see, the deaf hear, and the lame walk, even restoring dead people to life. He showed power over the forces of nature when He stilled the storm on Galilee, and when He fed over 5,000 people with five barley loaves and two fish.

Christ, in His life on earth, did His mighty works in the power of the Holy Spirit (Luke 4:1, 14; Matt. 12:28). In His incarnation Christ "emptied Himself of his equality with God (Phil. 2:6-7 NAS) and "became like man" (Phil. 2:7b TEV). It is easy to see that happen physically as He became a little baby in Mary's arms.

Christ chose to live by faith and according to the Scripture (Luke 4:18-21; Matt. 26:54,56). His entire life is an example of what it is like to live in the power of God.

After His death for our sins and His Resurrection by the Father, He was restored to His preincarnation glory. He announced that "All authority in heaven and on earth has been given to me" (Matt. 28:18 NIV). We read in Ephesians 1:20-21 that the Father "raised him from the dead and seated him at his right hand in the heavenly realms, far above all rule and authority, power and dominion, and every title that can be given, not only in the present age but also in the one to come. So Christ's power is greater than all other power.

Amazing as it seems, Christ has made His power available to us! Paul discovered this, appropriated it, and said "I can do everything through him who gives me strength" (Phil. 4:13 NIV). We do not know how Christ revealed that to Paul, but we do know that He gave Paul a "thorn in [the] flesh" (2 Cor. 12:7 NIV) to help him appropriate it. Paul prayed that those converted to Christ under his ministry would know by experience "the exceeding greatness of his power to us-ward who believe, according to the working of his mighty power" (Eph. 1:19 KJV).

We have the same assignment He gave them. We need the power they needed. Can we learn what they learned . . . to switch from our power to God's power? Please do not hear me saying that we will then find a trouble-free life and religious thrills. Those apostles were not severely persecuted until they switched to God's power. Then they were put in jail, beaten, stoned, and killed. Yet, they were truly and eternally successful.

**How do we make the switch?** Wake up to reality. God has all power. God wants us to serve, be stewards, and work for Him in His power. Recently, as I planted a tree, my neighbor's three-year-old son wanted to help me shovel the dirt. His little hands closed on the handle of the shovel and refused to turn loose. He put his foot on the shovel and tried to shove it into the ground, but it did not move. But I put my big foot on the other side of the shovel, supplied the power, and the shovel slid deep into the ground. He tried to lift the shovel full of dirt, but again he could not move it. I let him hold on while I supplied the power to lift the dirt out of the hole. He was jubilant! He called for his mother to see the hole he had dug. Being a grandfather at heart, I was made happy by his joy. I believe God wants to be involved in our daily lives like that. He wants to supply the power so we can be victorious in stewardship, and all of us will rejoice in the victory! Could it be that God allows us to bump up against our limited power so often because He is trying to show us we need to make the switch?

Decide to switch. Jesus called for that decision by giving His disciples the commands to serve, but to serve only in His power. The commands call for a decision. It is a little like switching on the light. The power company has the power ready, available, and waiting, but we must decide to flip the switch. This decision calls for self-denial. We are still too much like the child who says to his dad, "Let me do it by myself."

Obey His Word. The power comes when we obey, and not before. When the day of Pentecost came, when the harvest was ripe, when the 120 obeyed in prayer and willingness to witness . . . then God empowered them. When Peter was on trial before the same men who had tried Jesus, he was "filled with the Holy Spirit" (Acts 4:8 NIV) the moment he began to speak.

Trust God to supply the power. He told us not to worry about what to do or say when the time comes for action. He promised the Holy Spirit would supply all that we need. He is ready and waiting.

Abide in Christ!

The secret of successful stewardship is found in switching from our power to God's power!

## Reflections . . .

1. What can you do apart from Christ? Does your life demonstrate that you believe this?
2. Describe the difference between living in human power versus living in God's power.
3. This chapter lists six steps we can take to switch to God's power. List them. What steps do you need to take?

# Teaching
# Suggestions

This book is a resource in the Christian Growth Study Plan (formerly Church Study Course). To receive credit, attend a 2 ½ hour group study or for individual study, read the book, write answers to the Reflections sections, then show your work to your pastor, a staff member, or a leader in your church. For a request form and information about the Christian Growth Study Plan, refer to the current Christian Growth Study Plan Catalog. Someone in your church office may have a copy. If not, contact the Christian Growth Study Plan office, 127 Ninth Avenue North, MSN 117, Nashville, TN 37234-0117, phone (615) 251-2525.

**Group study:** For a 2 ½-hour study, allow an average of 15 minutes per chapter. If all participants have read the book, use the Reflections questions to guide the study. If not, use the chapter by chapter suggestions below.

## The Foundations of Stewardship
1. Use a poster of the ten chapter titles to introduce this study.
2. Discuss the idea of "proper management" (p. 5) and these three foundational truths of stewardship: God owns everything; God has entrusted some of His possessions to us; God holds us accountable.
3. Ask small groups to study and report on what the following Scriptures reveal about God's ownership of all things: Deuteronomy 8:11-18; Job 38-39; Romans 8:19-23. Ask these same small groups to discuss how bad stewards display the absence of a saving relationship with God.

## Trusted with a Body
1. Give all participants a blank sheet of paper. Ask them to make two lists: (1) the positive features of their body; (2) their least

favorite body features. Assure them that this is their personal list; they will not be asked to share it with anyone.
2. Ask people to find the seven actions (section headings) of body stewardship and list them on a chalkboard.
3. Discuss the similarity between the making of an Old Testament sacrifice and the presenting of the body as a living sacrifice; how Jesus used His body to glorify God; the possibility of to-day's Christians glorifying God in their bodies in death.

## Trusted with a Mind

1. Display on an overhead cell the six characteristics of the nat-ural mind (pp. 20-21). Ask participants to suggest examples of these characteristics.
2. Lead the group to form a definition or description of the spiri-tual mind.
3. Discuss selective forgetting and selective recall (p. 23).
4. Help the group identify our responsibilities in renewing our minds.
5. Have small groups study and report on one (or more) of the seven fibers of the "mind girdle."

## Trusted with an Ability

1. Ask the group to help you make two lists:
   a. common abilities with which a Christian can glorify God;
   b. uncommon abilities with which a Christian can glorify God.
2. Ask half the participants to read Romans 12:6-9, 1 Corinthians 12:8-10, and Ephesians 4:11 and identify body gifts mentioned. Ask the others to compose a list of gifts needed in your church.
3. Ask participants to discuss reasons why the lists are not exactly the same.

## Trusted with Time

1. Ask, Do we all have the same amount of time?
2. Lead the group in a discussion of "time" according to the Bible. Ask participants to compare that with current American think-ing on time management.
3. Assign two study groups:
   a. Group one will read and review Romans 13:12-14.
   b. Group two will report on why we are to redeem time.
4. Discuss the connection between good time stewardship and doing God's will.

## Trusted with Relationships

1. Write Our Cultural Heritage, Our National Heritage, Our Family Heritage, and Our Spiritual Heritage on posters. Ask participants to suggest ways we can be stewards of these.
2. Ask participants to list relationships in their lives (children, spouse, church, friends, etc.). Again, ask participants to suggest ways we can be good stewards of these relationships.

## Trusted with Possessions

1. Ask someone to be prepared to share a testimony of their stewardship pilgrimage in regarding possessions. Allow others to share if they wish.
2. Lead the group to discuss these questions:
   "Why should we honor God with our substance?"
   "How can we honor God with our substance?"

## Trusted with Position

1. As someone reads aloud 1 Peter 1:1-10, ask members to listen for ways God qualifies every believer to be a priest.
2. Provide enough copies of recent newspapers for each member of the group to have a front page section. Ask them to locate an article in which someone needs the ministry of a Christian priest. Ask each one to share briefly their article and describe how a "1 Peter 2" priest would minister.

## Trusted with the Gospel

1. Help the group understand the word gospel. Define the word, focusing on the description given in 1 Corinthians 15:1-4.
2. Ask, If we honestly accept our responsibility as trusted stewards of the gospel, how does it change our lives?

## Trusted with the Secret of Successful Stewardship

1. Ask, Can we be successful stewards without the power of Christ? After discussion, ask someone to read John 15:5.
2. Ask, What do we learn when we fail because we do not depend on God's power?
3. Close the study in prayer.